BASIC BIBLE SERIES

EPHESIANS

LIFE
IN THE
CHURCH

D1453746

BASIC BIBLE SERIES

EPHESIANS

LIFE
IN THE
CHURCH

DAVID C. COOK PUBLISHING CO.
ELGIN, IL 60120

Ephesians: Life in the Church

© 1986 David C. Cook Publishing Co., 850 North Grove Ave., Elgin, IL 60120. Printed in U.S.A.

Scripture quotations, unless otherwise noted, are taken from the Holy Bible: New International Version, © 1973, 1978, 1984 by the International Bible Society, used by permission of Zondervan Bible Publishers.

Design: Melanie Lawson
Cover: Dale Gottlieb
Compiled by: Deborah Barackman
Edited by: Gary Wilde

ISBN: 0-89191-480-3
Library of Congress Catalog Number: 86-70887

Being built together to become a dwelling in which God lives by his Spirit.

Contents

Introducing the Book of Ephesians

Authorship

The letter to the believers at Ephesus was written in A.D. 61 during Paul's imprisonment (under house arrest) in Rome. The letter was probably meant to be read and heeded in all the churches of the province of Asia, not just at Ephesus.

In the Book of Ephesians, Paul refers to himself as the "prisoner of Christ Jesus" (vs. 3:1), "prisoner for the Lord" (vs. 4:1), and an "ambassador in chains" (vs. 6:20). These are three hints about the status of his living arrangements.

Some have insisted that Paul could not have written Ephesians at all. Their reasoning lies in the difference in vocabulary and style as compared to other Pauline epistles. By comparison, there are over 70 new words in Ephesians. The style is more like that of a carefully planned treatise than a letter. Compared with some of his other epistles, it seems somewhat distant and impersonal.

But such differences are not so significant when we look at Paul's situation. Being a prisoner gave this "ambassador in chains" time to think, reflect, and evaluate what he wanted to say. This, coupled with Paul's intention that the letter be applicable to churches in a wide area, may help explain the change in style. Furthermore, Paul's mind was expansive and expressive, so much so that in saying new things—carefully thought out truths—he needed new words. Thus the difference in vocabulary and style does not give good reason for rejecting Pauline authorship.

Major Themes

In Ephesians, Paul was concerned with the sufficiency and centrality of Christ. All things unite in Him. However, because of the Fall, we experience a world that is anything but unified. Life is disharmonious and disjointed. Everywhere there is class consciousness, racial tension, national prejudice, and religious intolerance.

But Paul had caught the truly cosmic spirit of Christ's Gospel in this letter and was meticulously attempting to get it across. All the broken strands were knotted together again in Jesus as if they had never been severed from Creation. The middle wall of partition between Jew and Gentile had been broken down by the cross of Christ. Now *all* Christians are called to a new kind of "life in the Church" which moves in the direction of Christian maturity.

Paul also expressed this great idea of oneness in Christ when writing the Book of Colossians. This probably accounts for the similarity between the two writings. By one estimate, over 50 verses are virtually the same in the two epistles.

Ephesians can be divided into two major sections: doctrinal exposition in chapters 1—3, and the application of that doctrine to the Christian's life in chapters 4—6. Chapters 1—3 stress the believer's rich spiritual standing in Jesus Christ. They tell us who we are in Christ: part of one new Church, made of both Jew and Gentile, reconciled to God through Jesus' death and resurrection. Beginning with chapter 4, the apostle exhorted his readers to translate that spiritual wealth into daily living, drawing upon the strength of the empowered Body of Christ. We are to live (or "walk," vs. 4:1, KJV) in a way befitting our new status.

Paul's words were a source of much strength and encouragement to the original readers. In our day—with such anxious searching for true faith—the truth of Ephesians still stands. Jesus Christ is Lord of all. He alone deserves our worship, love, and daily devotion.

Destination

The city of Ephesus was among the most important religious centers in all Asia Minor. It was a crossroads of communication, commerce, and craftsmanship— especially the trades of silversmithing and image making (see Acts 19:23-28). Paul's audience consisted mainly of Gentiles, who lived in a pagan society without the moral standards of God's Law.

The cosmopolitan mood of Ephesus welcomed various philosophies and religions, most notably the cult of Diana, the Roman fertility goddess associated with the moon and hunting. (Diana's Greek name was Artemis.) Worshipers of Diana believed that she, along with other gods, exerted influence over humanity and that life could be more pleasant and profitable if they pleased her. Sacrifices were made to her for that reason.

Paul had faced demonic opposition while he ministered in Ephesus on his third missionary journey. Many of those who became Christians had practiced wicked deeds, including sorcery. Moreover, idolatry had a strong hold on western Asia Minor through the temple of Diana. Because the message of Christ called for a repudiation of idolatry and the immoral practices idolatry promoted, the silversmiths and other tradespeople tried to stamp out the Christian preachers. Paul's defense—partly preserved in Ephesians—was a key reason for the spread of Christianity.

Our society needs the Gospel as desperately as did the Ephesians. We live among people who worship a variety of gods—materialism, fame, security, comfort, convenience, self-fulfillment. And these gods are worshiped with sacrifices of time, money, and energy. If we, like Paul, challenge these "religions" and disturb those who have built their lives on such belief systems, we can expect opposition also. We can expect to be challenged from within, as our bent to sin resists the will of God. And, as the Holy Spirit begins to work His will in our lives, we will find ourselves out of step with others. Some may openly resent us for such differences. However, the benefits of a God-pleasing life-style far outweigh the discomforts.

In the first centuries, it has been said, the Christians out-thought, out-lived, and out-died their contemporaries. Because of words and truths such as those in Ephesians, they were able to do so.

Meditate on the Message of Ephesians!

Too often we read Scripture like the small boy or girl at Halloween who, under cover of darkness, sneaks up on the steps of a neighbor's porch, rings the doorbell, and watches, giggling, in the bushes.

The often missed key to profitable Bible study is *meditation:* giving the Holy Spirit the time He requires to get God's Scriptural messages through to us.

A passage like Ephesians 1 especially requires our meditation. Ring the doorbell and stand waiting for the door to open, and for God to invite you into His inner chambers.

1
Blessed Citizens

Truth to Apply: Citizenship in God's new community, the Church, brings me tremendous spiritual blessings.

Key Verse: Praise be to the God and Father of our Lord Jesus Christ, who has blessed us in the heavenly realms with every spiritual blessing in Christ (Eph. 1:3).

How does a person become a citizen of a country? One must be born in the country or have one parent who is already a citizen. Or one can apply for citizenship. News magazines regularly tell about tennis or ballet stars who have left their own countries to seek citizenship in the United States or Canada. Such people must apply for citizenship, study the history and the government of the new country, then pass an exam to become naturalized citizens.

None of these ways is the procedure for joining God's community. People are vastly ignorant about how God accepts citizens into His spiritual society. Most people (if they care at all) think good works earn acceptance with God. Some of these people are miserable, feeling they have never done enough. Others are rather blithely expecting that their misdemeanors aren't serious enough to bar Heaven's gates.

But there is nothing anyone can do to merit *spiritual citizenship*. You can't be born in the right place or study the right things. Yet God has made a way. In your own words, how would you explain the "plan"?

Background/Overview: *Ephesians 1:1-14*

Paul was writing to people he knew and loved. He had spent over two years teaching the Ephesian people (see Acts 19:8, 10) and a good deal of time establishing churches in other parts of Asia Minor. It is odd then that there are no personal greetings at the beginning of the letter. The reason may well be that this manuscript was intended to function as a circular letter for several churches in western Asia Minor. (Some important early manuscripts do not have "in Ephesus" in verse 1.) Some scholars suggest it may have been sent first to the Ephesian church, which, as a strong "mother church" for the area, would then have taken the responsibility to circulate it.

Since these people had been well taught, Paul doesn't repeat the details of the Crucifixion and Resurrection, but builds on these truths. Ephesians was written around A.D. 61 during Paul's first confinement in Rome when he was under house arrest. He also wrote Colossians, Philemon, and Philippians during this period. (You might find it helpful to read Colossians as you study the Book of Ephesians, since it parallels many of the same truths.)

Light on the Text

Greetings (1:1, 2)

1:1　As was customary, Paul identifies himself in the salutation of the letter. He calls himself an apostle of Jesus Christ. "Apostle" means "one who is sent" to do a special task. According to the verse, why was he an apostle? Paul clearly states that it was "by the will of God." He certainly hadn't asked to be an apostle. In fact, at the time God chose him, Paul was persecuting the believers! (See Acts 9.) But God selected him for the great mission of sharing the Gospel with the Gentiles. They were soon to have a marvelous truth revealed to them. This truth, which had been hidden for ages past, concerned God's plan to include them in His new society.

14

Notice what Paul calls these people to whom he writes: "saints." Today the word "saints" conjures up images of martyrs or super-holy people who are doing God's work in some remote, dreadful place. The actual New Testament meaning of the word, however, means someone dedicated to the distinctive possession and use of God. The Ephesian people surely understood this meaning, for many of the objects in the Temple of Diana were dedicated in the same way.

1:2 Notice the blessing Paul bestows on these beloved believers: "Grace and peace." This phrase is often linked together in Paul's writings, and it is understandable why he would do so. "Grace" is the unmerited favor of God and "peace" is the condition that results from receiving grace. There is a fellowship in St. Louis, Missouri, named "Grace and Peace." What a delightful name for a church! All believers will experience joy when meditating on the gifts of God's grace and peace.

God Takes the Initiative (1:3-14)

This section is a doxology—a spontaneous outpouring of worship to God—for the spiritual blessings He gives in Christ. Here unfolds the plan that gives us the great gift of spiritual citizenship.

1:3 Paul praises God for blessing "us in the heavenly realms with every spiritual blessing." "Heavenly realms" appears four other times in the letter (1:20; 2:6; 3:10; 6:12). It is the blazing, nonmaterial center of the universe where Christ rules. In this spiritual arena every being—good or evil—knows that Jesus is God. The blessings we now receive in Christ were previously enjoyed only by those who dwelt in Heaven with God. These blessings secure our acceptance with God.

1:4 Notice the first step God took to make us citizens. The verse says God "chose us." The wonder of it is not that humanity chooses God, but that God chooses us. And, more marvelous, God's plan for His spiritual community was activated before the world was even created.

But what were we chosen for? God's purpose in calling out a special people was that they be "holy and blameless" in His sight. The first of these words means "different." The Sabbath day was different from other days; therefore it was a holy day. The Christian is also to be different, identifiably distinctive in character. (Note the same root idea as in the word "saint.") "Blameless" carries the idea of being acceptable. We are acceptable— not because of anything we do or refuse to do—but because God has made us blameless in His Son. This refers not only to our legal standing before God, clothed in Christ's perfection, but also to the process of the working of His grace in cleaning up our lives, making us mature and more like Jesus.

1:5   Now the next step for spiritual citizenship: God arranged for us to be adopted into His family. God in love predestined us to be adopted "as his sons through Jesus Christ." The word "predestined" ties into the truth that this plan predated the foundation of the world. Paul is the only New Testament writer who uses the concept of adoption, but the practice was common in the Roman world. Masters who had no children would often adopt a slave or a slave's child as a son. This changed status gave the new son all the rights and privileges of a freeborn son. He was heir to all the father's blessings and possessions. People can't be born physically into spiritual citizenship, but they can be "reborn" through this adoption process. God's sole reason for doing this is that it was "in accordance with his pleasure and will." This is a mystery too deep to penetrate but it is no wonder that Paul fairly bursts with praise to God for this glorious grace so freely given.

1:7, 8   What, then, are the blessings that citizenship brings? 1) Redemption through Christ's blood; 2) the forgiveness of sins; 3) revelation of the mystery that all things are being brought under Christ's headship.

     "Redemption" is a tremendous word. When something is redeemed, something else is given for it. And that is exactly what happened on the Cross: we were redeemed. God gave His Son for us. He bore the penalty for our sins, paid our debt and set us free. (The adolescent

16

graffiti "Jesus Saves Green Stamps" has more truth in it than the youngsters realize, for aren't the places where shoppers go to exchange the stamps for gifts called Redemption Centers?) The price Jesus paid was infinite, His very life poured out in death. The transfer of sin to a blameless other was prefigured in the Old Testament sacrifices and the blood of the Passover lamb (see Ex. 12).

Redemption also carries the idea of buying back something that was owned before. Pawnshop transactions illustrate this process today. God owned us before we willfully rejected His control: Jesus' blood buys us back.

The Scope of Salvation (1:9-14)

1:9, 10 Paul can scarcely contain himself as he reflects on the riches and blessings God lavishes upon us, including spiritual and practical knowledge. Paul marvels at the outworking of God's plan through the ages and alludes to the drawing in of these Gentile believers as a great step toward bringing all things under Christ's headship. He will develop this theme fully later in the letter.

This oneness in Christ is the basis for the new community God is creating. When the "times will have reached their fulfillment," everything in Heaven and earth will be united in Christ. All history is hurtling toward this consummation. Today, Christ is the head of the Church. But someday He will be head of a completely redeemed Creation, when all will bow to His Lordship. The blessings we as Christians have in Christ are glorious, but there are even more to come.

1:11-14 Paul shows how the scope of the promise given the Jews has now been opened up to Gentile believers. In verse 11 he speaks as a Jewish believer (a converted Pharisee!) saying the Jewish people had also been chosen and numbered as those "who were the first to hope in Christ." (Jesus' disciples and most of His followers were all Jews.) God's purpose in choosing them was to bring praise to His glory. Paul then goes on to assure his Gentile readers (which means us as well), "And you also were included in Christ." When were they included in

Christ? When they heard the word of truth and joyfully believed it (see Acts 19). Paul calls this word of truth "the gospel [or good news] of your salvation."

God then puts a special mark on believers to claim them as His own. This mark or seal is the Holy Spirit Himself placed within us. A seal was a mark of authenticity or ownership, just as seals function on legal documents today. Not only is the presence of the Holy Spirit in our lives a sign that we are truly God's people, but it is also actually a first installment on the inheritance we are promised when God's cosmic purposes in redemption are completed. And this is all for "the praise of his glory."

John Stott has a letter opener with "for the praise of His glory" engraved on it. Such a daily reminder is a grand idea.

SPIRITUAL BLESSINGS IN CHRIST

Verse	Blessing	How God Gives Blessings in Christ
4	Chosen	He chose us *in him* before the creation of the world.
5	Adopted	He predestined us to be adopted as sons *through Jesus Christ.*
6	Grace given	His glorious grace, which he has freely given us *in the One he loves.*
7, 8	Redeemed	*In him* we have redemption through his blood, the forgiveness of sins, in accordance with the riches of God's grace.
9	God's will revealed	He made known to us the mystery of his will according to his good pleasure, which he purposed *in Christ.*
13a	Included	And you also were included *in Christ* when you heard the word of truth.
13b, 14	Sealed	Having believed, you were marked *in him* with a seal, the promised Holy Spirit.

For Discussion

1. What assurance does verse 13 give that these blessings of citizenship are for us as well as for the Ephesian

believers? Express how you feel about the blessings you are now receiving "in Christ."

2. What do people you know think makes them acceptable to God? What would you show them in this chapter to help change their thinking?

3. How does a deeper understanding of God's purposefulness in carrying out the process of salvation give *you* a greater sense of purpose? What practical things can you do to have more spiritual direction?

2
Enlightened Citizens

Truth to Apply: I can understand and use the spiritual resources God promises to all members of His new community, the Church.

Key Verse: I pray also that the eyes of your heart may be enlightened in order that you may know the hope to which he has called you, the riches of his glorious inheritance in the saints, and his incomparably great power for us who believe (Eph. 1:18, 19a).

There have been rich people who, because of paranoia or eccentricity, lived extremely pinched lives. At the end of his life, multimillionaire Howard Hughes became a suspicious hermit, using very little of his fortune. Newspapers tell of people all the time who die in squalor yet have large bank accounts. These people have riches but are unable to derive any pleasure from them.

Do most Christians behave this way when it comes to their spiritual riches in Christ? Why?

Most likely, Paul was a prisoner in Rome when he wrote the Letter to the Ephesians. He received illumination by the Holy Spirit concerning the great theme of divine redemption and the establishment of God's new community, the Church. Actually, the Ephesian epistle is more than a letter. It is a theological treatise that God gave Paul to strengthen the faith of the churches of Asia.

We have seen that Ephesians begins with an exposition of the purpose of God for the Church. In the first part of Ephesians 1, Paul praises God for His kindness in lavishing blessings upon us. But he directs the second part of the prayer toward the Ephesians—asking that they would know with their hearts as well as their minds what God has done. Paul wants us to know fully all the benefits spiritual citizenship brings. In Acts we see Paul taking full advantage of his Roman citizenship in his encounters with magistrates. In the same way, he wants Christians to use all the spiritual resources at their disposal.

Verses 15-23 begin with the apostle Paul praying for the new thing God has done in His world—the Church of Jesus Christ. In essence, Paul is praying for the community of believing Christians to experience the power that raised Jesus from the dead. In this way they can overcome sin and live as God wishes.

Light on the Text

Prayer for Friends (1:15-17)

1:15, 16 Paul has heard about the faith and love of these Christians. Each quality is essential to what it means to be a Christian. Faith in the Lord Jesus is the means by which we receive forgiveness, reconciliation, and adoption into the family of God. Love for all the saints necessarily follows from a right relationship with God.

But in spite of the good report, Paul has not stopped praying for them. He says he gives thanks for them and remembers them in his prayers. Here we see one of

Paul's secrets as a Christian leader: constantly upholding in prayer the people to whom he ministered. We could be much more effective if we followed Paul in this. Our relationships would be smoother if we remembered to thank God regularly for people.

1:17   Paul continues his prayer, asking God to give these people "the Spirit of wisdom and revelation." Several versions of the Bible capitalize "Spirit" to imply the Holy Spirit. Whether Paul meant this is somewhat uncertain, but receiving spiritual wisdom and revelation does involve the work of the Holy Spirit. We constantly need His quickening of our spirits to deepen our relationship with God.

God wants us to know Him personally. This is His purpose in giving wisdom and revelation. He doesn't want us just to know *about* His mighty acts and characteristics, but to truly know Him. We need only think of God's fellowship with Adam and Eve in the garden to see that this has always been His plan. He drew out His new community, the Church, for fellowship with Himself, and for the fellowship of each member with the others.

Three Sources of Strength (1:18-20)

Many Christians always seem to be defeated. In spite of their faith there is little evidence of real power or adequacy in their lives. They just drag on day after day without experiencing anything of the power that filled the early church. Paul's prayer shows us the way to break through this defeat.

1:18, 19   Paul prays that the eyes of the believers' hearts (their entire inward beings) be enlightened so they will know three specific things: 1) the hope to which He has called them; 2) the riches of His glorious inheritance in them; 3) His incomparably great power for them and all who believe. Often these days the word "hope" carries an element of doubt, as in "I hope it won't rain." But in Scripture "hope" means "strong confidence." Look back to verse 4 to see what the hope of our calling is. We were called by God to "be holy and blameless in his sight." Reflecting on this renews our sense of spiritual purpose.

God chose us for a definite reason and He will help us fulfill it. Philippians 1:6 gives the confident promise "that he who began a good work in you will carry it on to completion until the day of Christ Jesus." "The riches of his glorious inheritance in the saints" means there are even greater blessings to come. You'll remember from verse 14 that the indwelling Holy Spirit is our seal or guarantee of this inheritance. We can catch glimpses of these blessings by reading Revelation. It pictures crowds of worshipers, circling the throne of God, singing His praises. Only in Heaven will our fellowship with God be complete.

John Stott notes that the "hope of God's call" refers to the beginning of our Christian lives, while the "riches of his glorious inheritance" points to the end. God's "incomparably great power," therefore, is for the stretch of time in between—our Christian lives now!

1:19, 20   These verses say the power God used to raise Christ from the dead is available for all believers. No wonder the apostles spoke with such power in Acts! Note the adjectives Paul uses in verse 19 to describe this power: "incomparably" and "great." It seems Paul can't describe it strongly enough! (Scholar Marvin Vincent says this shows "Paul's intensity of style, and marks the struggle of language with the immensity of the divine mysteries . . . .") This power comes wholly from God. God's power helps us withstand our sinful society and gives assurance that we, too, will be resurrected.

Christ's Exaltation and Rule (1:21-23)

1:21   God demonstrated His power by exalting Christ to a position of highest authority. Christ is now sovereign over everything: demons, evil people, ideologies, governments. Desperate headlines about terrorism, threats of nuclear war, AIDS, and divorce sometimes make us forget that Christ rules in our present age as well as in the one to come. In II Peter 3:9 we have insight into why God lets evil events continue. God's purposes in bringing persons to salvation are still being worked out. But just as Christ was born "when the time had fully come" (Gal. 4:4), so, too, will history suddenly end.

1:22, 23   God placed everything under Christ's feet. (Psalm 110:1 prophesied this with the image of His enemies as His footstool.) Why was Christ given authority over everything? These verses tell us that it was for the Church. The thought that God directed His purpose toward His community of called-out believers should strike awe and wonder in our souls. Why He would choose us for such honor certainly is rooted in His mercy and not in our own worthiness. Once again we see the emphasis on God's grace.

Since Christ is now head (sovereign) for the sake of the Church, the Church shares what has come to Christ. We partake in Christ's ascension and exaltation to the right hand of the Father in Heaven. (Recall the promise in verse 3 that we have been blessed in the heavenly realms with every spiritual blessing in Christ.) Since Christ is victorious, so will His Church be.

God destined us for such an intimate relationship with Him, that the Church is called Christ's Body. Paul uses the image of the Church as the Body of Christ often in his letters. Christ is the head who directs the life and actions of His Body.

1:23   Most commentators understand verse 23 to mean that the Church contains the fullness of Christ. The Christ who fills the universe fills His Church in a special way. John 1:16 says, "From the fullness of his grace we have all received one blessing after another." In Colossians 2:10 Paul writes, "and you have been given fullness in Christ, who is the head over every power and authority." However, some noted scholars (including John Calvin) believe this passage teaches that the Church fills Christ. Just as the human torso "fills" out the head, the head/body imagery shows such an integral relationship that in this sense Christ chooses to have the Church fill Him. Later in Ephesians Paul compares the mystical union of Christ and His Church to marriage, calling it "a profound mystery."

As you meditate on the cascade of blessings in Ephesians 1 you may wish to personalize verses 17 and 18 of Paul's prayer: "Glorious Father, please give me a spirit of wisdom and revelation so that I may know You better. Please enlighten the eyes of my heart, so that I may know the hope to which You have called me, the riches of Your glorious inheritance in the saints, and Your incomparably great power for me. Amen."

For Discussion:

1. How can we draw more fully on God's "incomparably great power"?

2. How does considering yourself part of Christ's Body deepen your relationship with Him? How does it change your conception of the Church?

3. How has Paul's prayer been a model for your own prayer life? Do you have any current goals for your prayer life? Share.

3
Remade Citizens

Truth to Apply: God has totally remade me, and now calls me to a life of good works.

Key Verses: But because of his great love for us, God, who is rich in mercy, made us alive with Christ even when we were dead in transgressions (Eph. 2:4, 5a).

Before-and-after stories are a perennial feature in magazines and newspapers. Think of the kinds of articles you see over and over again. Weight loss testimonials, cosmetic and hairdo makeovers, and home remodeling projects are popular ones. Usually these articles focus on physical appearance, though some magazines chronicle bootstrap success stories.

Ephesians 2:1-10 tells the greatest before-and-after story ever. But this is one you're not likely to see in the popular press. The world doesn't understand spiritual makeovers. For example, it reacts skeptically to a claim like Cathy Crowell Webb's that her conversion caused her to seek justice for the man she'd falsely accused of rape. In your opinion, is such skepticism (about changed lives) justified?

Background/Overview: *Ephesians 2:1-10*

In the last chapter we saw that the end of Ephesians 1 is a prayer for us to gain greater knowledge of certain truths, particularly the power we have as it was displayed by God in raising Christ from the dead.

To apply this to us, Paul draws a parallel in Ephesians 2:1-10. As Christ physically died and rose from the dead, so the Ephesians were spiritually dead and have been raised by God. Paul goes on to show that as Jew and Gentile were united by God's act of heading up all things in Christ (Eph. 1:10-13), so they are now "one new man" (Eph. 2:15).

The passage contrasts the old life, ending in spiritual death, with the new life that God gives. Christ calls His people to renounce the old life and embrace the new life. One aspect of Christian teaching (found to some degree also in Judaism) was the demand for renunciation of the old life, repentance from sin, and a new pattern of behavior. A. D. Nock, in his book, *Conversion,* said Judaism and Christianity thus stood in sharp contrast to the pagan religions around them in their clear call to conversion; they were concerned with "a new life in a new people." Only spiritually remade people are fit for citizenship in God's new community, the Church.

Light on the Text

Dead to God (2:1-3)

We sometimes get too preoccupied with chapter divisions. Especially here in Ephesians 2, we must resist splitting off 2:1 from 1:23. There Paul was praying that his readers would see God's power exemplified in raising a physically dead Christ and seating Him in Heaven. By way of parallel, Paul now says his readers were also dead and, as he continues four verses later, were made alive (quickened, raised) with Christ and seated with Him because of being in union with Christ.

In Scripture, "death" never means annihilation. It is the "separation of a person from the purpose or use for which he was intended," as Bible scholar H. S. Miller puts it. Scripture speaks of physical death, the separation of the soul from the body (I Cor. 15:21, 22); spiritual death, the separation of the spirit from God (as here in Eph. 2:1); and eternal death, eternal separation from God (II Thess. 1:9).

Spiritual death is the condition that all people without Christ find themselves in. Though Paul directs verse 1 to the Ephesians, he quickly moves on in verse 3 to say that "all of us" lived to gratify our sinful lusts and so were, in fact, "by nature objects [deserving] of wrath." Paul expands on humanity's debased condition in the first three chapters of Romans. In God's eyes anyone without His new life within is marked a dead person.

The Ephesians could remember the old life of spiritual death. It did involve a rather lively way of life. Fulfilling every lustful desire of flesh and mind usually leads to a whirlwind life-style: "living in the fast lane." Such a course is so lively (in sin) that it is deadly. However, even the most outwardly genteel people pursue their own self-centered desires and are totally dead to any relationship with God. Without God, one is in cultural bondage to this world's way of thinking and acting.

Who empowers those who are spiritually dead? Verse 2 teaches that they follow "the ways of this world" because Satan is at work in them, spurring on their willful disobedience to God. God has allowed Satan temporarily to command the spiritual forces influencing humankind for evil. In John 14:30 Christ calls Satan "the prince of this world." These verses show the truth in the cliché, "the world, the flesh and the devil," as sources for sin. Societal influences, our own sinful desires, and Satan's active work are all death dealing.

Made Alive by Grace (2:4, 5)

The previous verses lay out a desperate situation; then like a trumpet blast verses 4 and 5 sound a high note of hope. "But because of his great love for us, God, who is rich in mercy, made us alive with Christ even when we were dead in transgressions—it is by grace you have been saved." The picture quickly shifts from past despair to present optimism.

Mercy, love, and grace are essential aspects of God's character. We see these at work in all of God's dealings with His people, most profoundly in God's relationship with Israel according to the Old Testament.

MERCY	LOVE	GRACE
Ps. 103:8	Hos. 14:4	Ex. 34:6
Lam. 3:22	Deut. 7:7	Joel 2:13
Jonah 3:12	Mal. 1:2, 3	Jonah 4:2

We see mercy at work in such synonyms as "compassionate," "loving-kindness," and "gracious." Mercy has been called "God's attitude toward the lawbreaker and the rebel." Not only is God merciful, He is "rich in mercy."

Love is a noble term, indicating "the deep and constant love and interest of a perfect Being toward entirely unworthy objects" (Hogg and Vine). God's love is not merely an emotional response, it is an intelligent act of God's will for our welfare. Again we see that God not only is loving, He has "great love for us." The Old Testament shows God's love in choosing Israel for His people. God's love is always given freely (Hos. 14:4).

Not content with pointing to mercy and love as causes of our salvation, Paul introduces his favorite word, "grace." As we saw in 1:7, this loving grace is the ultimate reason for our salvation. All is of grace because we were all dead. Spiritual life is wholly a gift from God given while we were still dead in our transgressions. God's graciousness is a theme that pervades the Old Testament. It is often expressed in the phrase, "the compassionate and gracious God, slow to anger, abounding in love" (Ex. 34:6; Joel 2:13; Jonah 4:2).

Seated in the Heavenly Realms (2:6, 7)

Not only did God raise us from spiritual death with the same power that He raised Christ from physical death, but He has also seated us with Himself in the heavenly realms in Christ Jesus. Ephesians 1:3 said we were "blessed . . . in the heavenly realms." One of these blessings is to be spiritually seated with Christ at God's right hand. We partake in the victory that Christ's authority signifies. We are also joined in fellowship with Christ. What was God's chief reason for accomplishing this in us? Verse 7 explains that our salvation is to be a continual display throughout the ages of the "incomparable riches of his grace." We are to be an eternal testimony to the kindness (mercy) God showed us in Christ Jesus!

Looking back to 1:21 we see that every being in the spiritual realm knows what God has accomplished. And when God's purposes in history are completed, every human being will also acknowledge what God has done.

Grace Notes (2:8, 9)

Paul returns to his favorite theme, grace. Salvation is of necessity a gracious gift from God. Dead people cannot save themselves; therefore pride cannot get a foothold. We contribute nothing to our salvation. God's grace saves us through faith (our response). When Paul says "and this not from yourselves," he is referring to the entire process of salvation.

Salvation has its source neither in the human heart nor in human performance ("not by works"). No, salvation is all of grace. We cannot boast of a good heart, perfect actions, or spiritual insight. Grace saved us while we were still dead and repugnant in our sin.

Created to Do Good Works (2:10)

Notice what Paul calls the people whom God has regenerated. He says these remade citizens are "God's workmanship." We have been created in Christ Jesus for a purpose. What is it? God made us members of His spiritual community in order to do good works. Verses 8 and 9 emphatically declare that we cannot become saved by any good works on our part, but, after God makes us new creatures, He expects us to do good works. In fact, as verse 10 states, He has prepared specific works for us to do. Many people sincerely want to find God's will. This verse clearly teaches that God has a purposeful life planned for us. Claiming such promises is an excellent approach for spiritual guidance.

Dead in Sin		Alive in Christ	
Vs. 2a	followed the ways of this world	Vs. 5	by grace we have been saved
Vs. 2b	followed ruler of the kingdom of the air	Vs. 6a	raised us up with Christ
Vs. 3a	gratified cravings of our sinful nature	Vs. 6b	seated us with him in the heavenly realms in Christ Jesus
Therefore:		**Therefore:**	
Vs. 3b	we were by nature objects of wrath	Vs. 10	we are God's workmanship

For Discussion

1. What modern attitudes and actions illustrate what Paul describes as living in sin?

2. How does contemplating the reality of God's wrath affect your commitment to evangelism?

3. What sort of works do you believe God has prepared for you to do? How might you seek His direction?

4
Added Citizens

Truth to Apply: Citizenship in God's new community joins me to the heritage of the Jewish people.

Key Verses: Remember that at that time you were separate from Christ, excluded from citizenship in Israel and foreigners to the covenants of the promise, without hope and without God in the world. But now in Christ Jesus you who once were far away have been brought near through the blood of Christ (Eph. 2:12, 13).

South Africa's apartheid structure has bitterly divided the races. Some of the reasons for this division are: background (Western European vs. native African), wealth, education, race, religion, and political power.

In New Testament times, similar factors divided the Jews from the Gentiles: 1) Religion—the Jews followed the one true God while the Gentiles at Ephesus worshiped pagan gods, especially the goddess Artemis (Diana). More educated Gentiles looked to their philosophers for life's meaning. 2) Race—the Jews were a dispersed Semitic people, while the Gentiles were members of the Roman Empire. 3) Background—The Jewish nation claimed a long history of covenantal relationship with God, while the Gentiles had no such national calling.

Just as in South Africa today, these differences bred misunderstanding and hostility. How can such barriers be broken down in our modern world? How have they been broken down in the spiritual realm?

Background/Overview: *Ephesians 2:11-16*

The controversy over Jewish/Gentile relations was a major conflict in the fledgling Church. Peter's struggle at Joppa (Acts 10), the decision of the Jerusalem Council (Acts 15), Paul's letter to the churches of Galatia, and his arrest in Jerusalem (Acts 22) show the depth of concern people had about this perplexing question. Though Luke's Gospel shows that Christianity was destined to be a universal faith from the beginning (see particularly chaps. 1 and 2), the early followers of Jesus did not immediately grasp or easily accept this.

Paul understood that his calling was to be a minister to the Gentiles (Eph. 3:6, 7). The mystery of God now revealed by the Holy Spirit to the apostles was that the gift of Christ is for all people; the provisions of God's grace cannot be limited by national, cultural, or racial boundaries. God's new community, the Church, was to be universal (as the Apostles' Creed affirms: "a holy catholic Church"). As such it would show the "manifold wisdom of God" to "the rulers and authorities in the heavenly realms" (Eph. 3:10).

Paul's concern in Ephesians is not only to bridge the chasm between Jew and Gentile but to insist that his readers understand that the privileges of citizenship are both personal and social. As we saw in the last chapter, the first ten verses in Ephesians 2 focus on personal experience. We were all once dead in our sins, disobedient to the laws of righteousness, determined to satisfy our own lusts, and depraved by nature. But God in His mercy gave His Son so that by grace through faith we have been saved. Our transformation has made us the workmanship of God.

The present passage, Ephesians 2:11-16, relates to the social significance of the Gospel for the Gentiles. Previously they were aliens from the commonwealth of Israel, but now they are included in the family of God—heirs, together with the Jews, of God's promises. God's plan for His new community was to break down the barrier between the races and unite them into "one new man."

Light on the Text

Past Alienation (2:11, 12)

The word "Gentile" sounds innocent enough to us in the twentieth century. We cannot sense the disdain with which a Jew spat out the word. There were Jews and there were *goyim*. The *goyim* (the Hebrew equivalent of the Latin word "nations," from which we derive "Gentile") were the other people, the outsiders, the non-Jews. They were to be avoided. Paul reminds his Gentile readers that they long were "excluded from citizenship in Israel and foreigners to the covenants of the promise." They lived apart from the true God and knew nothing of His promised Messiah. Paul did not want them to forget their former distance from God's mercy. They were "separate from Christ" and "without hope and without God in the world." As verses 1-10 reminded them of their past sinful lives and allegiance to Satan, these verses underscore their alienation from God. Their gods were no gods. Even in their own mythologies these gods were more like capricious humans. So their religion offered no hope. The mystery religions that many Gentiles embraced often involved bloody cleansing ceremonies but could offer no promise of an eternal afterlife. Many of their philosophers rejected the concept of an afterlife altogether.

The Jews, rather than trying to be "a light for the Gentiles" as commanded in Isaiah 49:6, disdained the Gentiles, calling them the "uncircumcised." Circumcision was the religious sign that set apart the Jews from other people. The whole issue over whether Gentile men should be circumcised to demonstrate their faith became a much debated issue in the early church. Paul fought this rigorously, teaching that membership in God's new community did not make Jews out of Gentiles but rather made "one new man" from them both. The seal of this new community was the indwelling Holy Spirit (Eph. 1:13). Even in the Jewish nation, outward circumcision never assured a right relationship with God—that required "circumcision of the heart, by the Spirit" (Rom. 2:29).

Points of Alienation	Parallels in Our Society
1. Separate from Christ	1. "Jesus" is more often a swearword than a personal reality.
2. Excluded from citizenship in Israel	2. Lack of interest keeps many from the church.
3. Foreigners to the covenants of the promise	3. Lack of interest keeps many from reading the Bible.
4. Without hope	4. High substance abuse and suicide rates; nihilism in philosophy and literature.
5. Without God in the world	5. Apathy breeds a de facto atheism. Substitute gods are success, sex, money.

Present Peace (2:13, 14)

Just as Ephesians 2:4 followed its litany of despair about the Gentiles' sinful past with the triumphant "But God," so verse 13 begins with the uplifting "But now in Christ Jesus." Mournful minor chords suddenly swell to a glorious crescendo. What has Christ Jesus done for the Gentiles? He has brought near those who were once far away. J. B. Phillips translates: "You who were once outside the pale [enclosure or safeguard] are with us inside the circle of God's love." Christ accomplished this through the shedding of His blood on the cross, thereby gaining redemption for humankind. We saw in Ephesians 1:7, "In him we have redemption through his blood, the forgiveness of sins."

Paul then employs a beautiful description of Christ in verse 14, "For he himself is our peace." Isaiah 9:1-6 foretold that the Prince of Peace would bring a great light on the people walking in darkness—Jew and Gentile alike. Redemption insures peace with God. We were by nature "objects of wrath" deservedly bringing God's anger upon ourselves by our sinful lusts and cavalier disregard of Him. When by faith we accept Christ's atoning blood, we become "holy and blameless" in God's sight and are at peace with Him.

Christ's death not only brings peace to our relationship with God but also works to heal our relationships with others. Verse 14 teaches that the hostility between Jew and Gentile was forever destroyed. Instead of two warring peoples, the two have been made one. The image of a dividing wall of hostility probably refers to the layout of the Jewish Temple in Jerusalem. God-fearing Gentiles could only enter the outer Court of the Gentiles to worship the living God. A wall prevented them from entering the inner courts and partaking fully in the sacrificial worship. Indeed, the wall had an inscription on it that read: "No man of another nation may enter within the fence and enclosure round the temple. Whoever is caught will have himself to blame for his ensuing death." But when Christ's sacrifice was offered once for all, the walls in worship were torn down. All people could now boldly approach God. Hebrews 10:19, 20 teach that Jew and Gentile alike can "have confidence to enter the Most Holy Place by the blood of Jesus, by a new and living way opened for us through the curtain, that is, his body."

Notice the words and phrases in verses 12-16 that indicate loss and alienation:

Exclusion	Inclusion
Vs. 12 "separate"	Vs. 13 "brought near"
Vs. 12 "excluded"	Vs. 14 "made the two one"
Vs. 12 "foreigners"	Vs. 14 "destroyed the barrier"
Vs. 12 "without"	Vs. 16 "reconcile"
Vs. 14 "hostility"	Vs. 14 "peace"

Reconciliation Reigns (2:15, 16)

The Gospel is a Gospel of peace because it is a message of reconciliation. The death of Christ abolished the Law with its commandments and regulations in order to join Jew and Gentile into "one new man." Commentator William Barclay points out that the Greek word for "new" refers not to time but to quality. Both Jew and Gentile are qualitatively different; both are new creations.

The phrase "abolishing . . . the law with its commandments and regulations" does not mean, of course, that God is not concerned about holy living. Indeed, Ephesians 1:4 teaches that He chose us to be holy. God's Law showed how miserably we failed to obey Him. It functioned as a teacher to lead us to Christ (Gal. 3:24, 25). Romans 3:21 teaches that salvation brings a righteousness from God that is apart from the Law. This means we now obey God because of our relationship with Him rather than because a heavy yoke of rules has been laid upon us.

Christ's death reconciled to God both the Jews who had the Law and the Gentiles who were without the Law. The natural result of reconciliation to God was reconciliation with each other. Christ's cross, therefore, "put to death their hostility." The Church of Christ, which has been given the message of reconciliation (II Cor. 5:19), must not be stained by divisions based on race, gender, class, or nation.

For Discussion

1. In our churches, how can Jesus be "our peace"?

2. What are some practical ways we can begin to reach out to Christians with whom we differ?

3. What are some concrete strategies for reaching people who are without hope and without God in the world?

5
Fellow Citizens

Truth to Apply: I am a part of the one holy temple started when God joined Jewish and Gentile believers together in His new community.

Key Verses: Consequently, you are no longer foreigners and aliens, but fellow citizens with God's people and members of God's household, built on the foundation of the apostles and prophets, with Christ Jesus himself as the chief cornerstone (Eph. 2:19, 20).

Rising suddenly from a wheat field near Paris, Chartres Cathedral overwhelms its viewers with majesty. In some mysterious way, this great cathedral seems to radiate the devotion that built it.

Kenneth Clark, in *Civilisation*, says that when the cathedral was built in 1144 A.D. the faithful harnessed themselves to carts in order to drag stone from the quarry. Other men and women carried heavy provisions of wine, oil, and corn great distances to the workmen. Lords and ladies pulled carts along with the rest. Clark describes the reverent atmosphere: "There was perfect discipline and a most profound silence. All hearts were united and each man forgave his enemies."

Ephesians goes even deeper, picturing a harmonious people as the actual elements of a temple being built for God's habitation. In what ways is the Church today functioning harmoniously? How about your own local church?

Among the rabbis in New Testament times, the word "brother" referred to "an Israelite by blood"; the word "neighbor" meant "a proselyte" (a Gentile who had chosen to become a member of Israel). Neither of these titles was used to designate a Gentile as such.

In the New Testament, "brother" is frequently used to mean "fellow Christian." This involved more than fellow Jews, since, from the earliest days of the Church, the barriers were crossed to include non-Jews in the fellowship. God took some dramatic steps to teach the Jewish Christians that this was His will. Perhaps the most striking example is the vision He gave the apostle Peter at Joppa (Acts 11:9). A sheet descended from Heaven containing ritually clean and unclean animals. God's command to eat the unclean animals taught Peter that God now accepted the Gentiles as clean.

Galatians 3:26-29 teaches, "You are all sons of God through faith in Christ Jesus, for all of you who were baptized into Christ have clothed yourselves with Christ. There is neither Jew nor Greek, slave nor free, male nor female, for you are all one in Christ Jesus. If you belong to Christ, then you are Abraham's seed, and heirs according to the promise." Every distinction that could cause divisions among people is done away by the unity Christ brings. Spiritual citizenship granted the Gentiles all the blessings the Jews had experienced.

Paul had previously described God's act (of uniting Jew and Gentile) as destroying the dividing wall of hostility. On this rubble God chose to build these fellow citizens into a new temple. The Holy Spirit now dwelt within God's people. They become God's temple. Now Paul will explain what this new relationship means.

Light on the Text

Equal Access (2:17, 18)

Christ came and preached peace to "you who were far away" (the Gentiles) and peace to "those who were near" (the Jews). He bought this peace with His own blood (vs. 13). What did this peace bring? Christ's death gives both Jews and Gentiles access to the Father by the Holy Spirit. In the Old Testament, only the high priest could bring the sins of the people before God for atonement. Christ's once-for-all atoning sacrifice (which the Old Testament sacrifices foreshadowed) meant that all people could now come directly into God's presence. Christ Himself functions as our High Priest in Heaven, so we are welcome. Hebrews 10:22 says, "Let us draw near to God with a sincere heart in full assurance of faith, having our hearts sprinkled to cleanse us from a guilty conscience." In Ephesians 3:12 Paul stresses that in Christ we may approach God with "freedom and confidence."

The Holy Spirit is the active agent in bringing a person to God. We would never desire to enter God's presence if it were not for the Holy Spirit drawing us. As Jesus told Nicodemus, only the Holy Spirit can bring spiritual birth (Jn. 3:6). Ephesians 2:18 therefore clearly shows the involvement of all three Persons of the Godhead in our salvation.

GOD THE FATHER
(Access in fellowship)

JESUS CHRIST
(High Priest's atonement secured the forgiveness of our sins)

THE HOLY SPIRIT
(Drew us to God and gave new birth; witnesses to our spirits that we belong to God)

Equal Benefits (2:19)

Paul makes clear what is the result, for the Gentiles, of Christ's peacemaking. They are no longer foreigners and aliens; now they have become fellow citizens with God's people—indeed, members of God's household. These

Gentiles, who by their birth were cut off from membership in Israel, suddenly had a radical change in status! Through faith in Christ their relationship to God was changed. They had been separated from the Old Testament people of God, but now were a vital and integral part of the New Testament people of God. No longer could they be considered strangers or visitors. They now qualified as citizens of God's new community and members of the family of God.

A Holy Temple (2:20-22)

For the second time in two chapters Paul describes the Church. In chapter 1, he referred to it as the Body of Christ. As such it is to be subject to the head and filled with "the fullness of him who fills everything in every way" (Eph. 1:23).

Now Paul changes the metaphor to a building. The Church has become the temple of God. We are reminded of Paul's words to the Christians at Corinth: "Don't you know that you yourselves are God's temple and that God's Spirit lives in you?" (I Cor. 3:16). As a building, the Church requires a foundation and a superstructure. The superstructure is all of us who name the name of Christ. Peter uses this same image, "You also, like living stones, are being built into a spiritual house" (I Pet. 2:5).

A missionary to Afghanistan told how hostile Muslim government forces tore down one of the local churches so that not even one stone stood on another. "But," he said, "they couldn't touch the living stones, the people of God." The persecution only served to strengthen that Christian Afghan community.

The foundation has been laid by the apostles and prophets, according to verse 20. The reference to the apostles and prophets is not to these people personally, but to their ministry. In Ephesians 3, Paul says that the mystery of God (that is, the inclusion of the Gentiles in the divine redemptive purposes) "was not made known to men in other generations," but now it has been "revealed by the Spirit to God's holy apostles and prophets" (Eph. 3:5). This revelation serves as the basis for the development of the Christian Church.

Many theologians and Bible scholars maintain that our Christian faith rests on encounter with Christ alone, not on some book claiming to be divinely inspired. Paul believed that not only is there a verbal revelation from God, but such revelation is absolutely essential to our knowledge of God's purposes. What the prophets and apostles wrote is foundational to our faith.

Christ is the chief cornerstone. In modern buildings a cornerstone is a rather ornamental addition, but it was critical in ancient times. It was the stone around which the rest of the building was organized. This image therefore emphasizes the supreme significance of Jesus Christ for His Church. Isaiah 28:16 (which Peter quotes in his first epistle) prophesied of Christ: "See, I lay a stone in Zion, a tested stone . . . the one who trusts will never be dismayed."

As the cornerstone gave the building its structure, so in Christ "the whole building is joined together." His life fills His Church, breaks down barriers, and unites the members. Paul then teaches the Ephesian Christians that they are being built together to become a dwelling in which God's Spirit lives. Note that God does not dwell in us simply as individuals, but that God dwells in His Church. The indwelling Christ, who unites us, also dwells in us individually, but He does so because we are part of his Body, the Church. Paul is certainly not trying to deny the individual's relationship to God. But He is primarily interested in stressing our corporate relationship to God as part of the Church.

For Discussion

1. How can you be sure that you are building on the right foundation? How do you build on the apostles and prophets?

2. What measures can you take to view your church membership more seriously? How can you strengthen your sense of being a corporate part of "a holy temple in the Lord"? Give specific examples.

3. Do you draw on your privileges of access to God? How?

6

Revealed Citizens

Truth to Apply: I am personally involved in a great divine plan for the people of God.

Key Verse: His intent was that now, through the church, the manifold wisdom of God should be made known to the rulers and authorities in the heavenly realms (Eph. 3:10).

Are you a mystery fan? Perhaps as a child you devoured the Nancy Drew or Hardy Boy series. Now you've graduated to Dorothy Sayers's Lord Peter Wimsey or G. K. Chesterton's Father Brown series. What are some of the stock elements in a mystery story?

In mystery stories the answer is always revealed at the end. However, common usage of the word "mystery" is somewhat different. It usually means "unknown," with no assurance that an answer will ever be found. For example, the events surrounding the death of Jimmy Hoffa may always remain a mystery.

The connotation of the word "mystery" (*mysterion*) in classical and Biblical Greek was quite different. In classical Greek it meant "hidden or secret" (rather than unknown). Its plural form referred to the sacred rites in the Greek mystery cults. The New Testament uses the word to mean a secret in the process of being revealed, or which has already been revealed. The mystery is a divine secret that God has chosen to keep hidden until the proper time. It is a "temporary secret," which has become an "open secret."

In Ephesians 1:1-13 Paul uses "mystery" four times to describe God's creation of the Church. We will see what some of the Old Testament clues were and why this was the appropriate time for God to make this secret known.

Paul draws on some biographical information to explain his commissioning by God to reveal this mystery. He begins the passage by calling himself "the prisoner of Christ Jesus for the sake of you Gentiles." This was literally true: Paul was in prison because of what he was proclaiming to the Gentiles.

Acts 21:27-36 gives the details. Paul had returned to the church in Jerusalem to give a missionary report. While there, he went through some purification rites at the Temple. Some Jews from Asia saw him in the Temple and became enraged. They seized Paul, shouting, "This is the man who teaches all men everywhere against our people and our law and this place." They also accused him of bringing Gentiles into the Temple and defiling it. (Paul actually hadn't done this.) This was unthinkable to the unbelieving Asian Jews. To them, Paul was a traitorous and dangerous heretic. They tried to kill him on the spot, and only the intervention of the Roman authorities saved him. In a scene reminiscent of Jesus' crucifixion, the crowd shouted, "Away with him!" Paul drew on his Roman citizenship to exact the promise of a trial in Rome. When Paul reached Rome he was placed under house arrest, awaiting trial. He wrote the letter to the Ephesians during this imprisonment.

Light on the Text

Imprisoned for Christ (3:1)

Religious rivalry led to Paul's imprisonment, but ultimately Paul sees God's sovereign will at work. Thus he calls himself "the prisoner of Christ Jesus."

Notice that the apostle saw himself more as Jesus' prisoner than Caesar's. The Roman emperor had no power over him other than that allowed by King Jesus! Being a prisoner was part of the Lord's will to be used for His glory in spite of what Caesar might think.

Paul intended to record a prayer for his beloved Gentiles and so begins, "For this reason . . . ." In chapter 1 he followed a doctrinal explanation with a prayer. He desired here to conclude his teaching (on the oneness of the Gentiles' citizenship with the Jews) with a prayer also.

He doesn't actually get to his prayer until verse 14, however, because his use of the word "Gentiles" triggers a wish to explain to them more fully the eternal scope of God's plan for the Church.

The Mystery Revealed (3:2-6)

3:2-4   Paul again makes a biographical reference when he says, "Surely you have heard about the administration of God's grace that was given to me for you." He is alluding to his dramatic encounter with Jesus Christ on the Damascus Road, recorded in Acts 9 and Acts 22:3-21. Paul was told prophetically by Ananias that God had chosen Paul to know His will. Later, the Lord told Paul that He would send him to the Gentiles.

Paul had just briefly explained to his Gentile readers the nature of this new community, the Church. He had used the term "mystery" in Ephesians 1:9, but hadn't sketched out in detail the eternal nature of God's plan. This mystery was not something of his own making. Indeed, it was not a new thing at all—rather it was a revelation from God of an eternally existing idea, developed before "the creation of the world" (Eph. 1:4). Christ confronted Paul on the Damascus Road with the new concept of His Lordship and the Church. Then, as Paul studied for three years in Damascus and Arabia following his conversion, God no doubt revealed to Paul the sweep of His plan for the Church.

Paul says two things about the timing of God's revelation of this mystery: 1) It was not made known to men in other generations; 2) It has now been revealed by the Spirit to God's holy apostles and prophets.

Paul's statement, that the drawing in of the Gentiles was not made known to people in Old Testament times, has confused some commentators because God clearly prophesied that the Gentiles would become part of His people. What these commentators fail to consider, however, is that the mystery centers on the nature of the Christian Church. This totally new entity put Gentiles and Jews on equal footing before God. It is now the Church that is God's "holy nation" (I Pet. 2:9) rather than the nation of Israel. God was replacing His theocracy (a God-ruled, individual nation) with the Church—a called-out people of God who span every nation, every race, every culture. God opened the way for a global citizenry!

A LIGHT FOR THE GENTILES

It is exciting to trace the hints of this mystery as it was revealed to the Old Testament prophets:

l.	Gen. 12:1-3	All peoples blessed through the Jews
2.	Ps. 2:8	The nations will be the Son's inheritance
3.	Isa. 2:2-5	All nations will stream to the mountain of the Lord's Temple
4.	Isa. 11:10	The root of Jesse (Jesus, as David's descendent) will stand as a banner for the peoples; the nations will rally to Him
5.	Isa. 42:6	Israel to be a light for the Gentiles
6.	Isa. 49:6	Jews, as a light to Gentiles, to bring salvation to the ends of the earth
7.	Joel 2:28	God will pour out His Spirit on all people
8.	Zech. 8:21-23	Many peoples and powerful nations will come to Jerusalem to seek the Lord Almighty

3:5 God chose not to reveal this mystery in its fullness until Christ's reconciling work on the cross had actually been accomplished. Only then could all the barriers between God and humanity, and between Jew and Gentile, be broken. Only then could God's international community be organized. And only then could this people be seen as so completely holy and blameless that they could be united to Christ's Body.

When Paul says that this mystery has now been revealed by the Spirit to God's holy apostles and prophets, he refers indirectly to the inspiration of the New Testament Scriptures. He, Peter, John, James, and the other New Testament writers wrote God's very Word under the direction of the Holy Spirit. The words weren't dictatated, of course, but the Holy Spirit influenced their thinking in such a way that they truly recorded God's thoughts. II Peter 1:21 states: "For prophecy never had its origin in the will of man, but men spoke from God as they were carried along by the Holy Spirit." In II Timothy 3:16 we learn that "all Scripture is God-breathed."

3:6   The mystery of the Gospel grants three things to the Gentiles. They are now heirs together with Israel, members together of one Body, and sharers together in the promise of Christ Jesus. These are the points Paul carefully taught in Ephesians 2:11-22. To make them hit home even more strongly, Paul uses the Greek prefix "syn," which means "together with," for all these phrases. Translator J. Armitage Robinson translates these words, "co-heirs, concorporate, co-partakers." This gives us a stronger feel for the shared privileges of citizenship God has granted us. No longer do Gentiles have to ceremonially become Jews to experience God's covenant promises. Now all the members of Christ's Body, the Church, enjoy these blessings equally.

The Mystery Proclaimed (3:7-13)

The first part of chapter 3 concerned the message of the mystery given Paul by God. This section centers on the commissioning of Paul by God to preach this message. Preaching was for Paul the inevitable outcome of receiving these great truths. The truths of the Gospel are not solely for our private meditation and wonder, but "good news" to be told to unbelievers.

Paul could not get over the tremendous privilege granted him to be a minister of the Gospel. He had been chosen, not because he was worthy, but because of the free grace of God. For reasons unknown to Paul, the sovereign Lord had selected him to perform this job of Gospel proclamation. It always sobered and humbled him to think about it. Because of his previous history as a persecutor of Christians, Paul always thought of himself as the least worthy of all the people of God. To think that God would forgive him and call him to service in this manner was too much to comprehend. It was incredibly wonderful. Paul was nothing, and Christ was everything! That was not modesty; it was just the truth.

3:10, 11 Now Paul details the purpose for the Church. What does he say God's intent was? God created the Church in order that "the manifold wisdom of God should be made known to the rulers and authorities in the heavenly realms." "Manifold" literally means "multicolored." Christ's Church is certainly this, with representatives from every tribe and nation! Angelic beings look on amazed as God draws worshipers from every part of the world and gives them the inestimable privilege of union with Christ. "Rulers and authorities" may also refer to the wicked angels for whom this pageant is an open show of Christ's victory (see Col. 2:15).

The wisdom of God has been made known in the life, death, and resurrection of Jesus. Through the Gospel of Christ, the Church proclaims: God welcomes all races, classes, and nations!

Free Approach to God (3:12)

Paul repeats his teaching from Ephesians 2:18 that Christ's death provided free access to God. Much Old Testament history emphasized that God's mercy seat was unapproachable. People were struck dead if they dared to touch the Ark of the Covenant. The veil of forbidden access was draped across the entrance to the Holy of Holies. No one was allowed to enter except the High Priest, and only on the Day of Atonement (*Yom Kippur*).

Not until Jesus died on the cross was that veil torn away and a way opened to everyone through Him. He is now our High Priest, who makes intercession for all believers. This open access to God is what the 16th-century reformers called "the priesthood of all believers." We no longer need any mediator with God but Jesus. Christ Himself began to teach His disciples of this coming intimacy with God by teaching them to pray to "Our Father" and by changing their status from servants to friends (Jn. 15:14, 15).

Suffering and Glory (3:13)

Paul concludes this digression by reminding his friends not to be discouraged over his situation. He saw his own sufferings as being for the glory of the Gentiles. John Stott writes, "Paul is suffering in prison on their behalf, as their champion, standing firm for their inclusion in God's new society. So convinced is he of the divine origin of his vision that he is prepared to pay any price to see it become a reality" (*God's New Society*, p. 129).

For Discussion

1. Do you feel you can approach God with freedom and confidence? If not, what are some of the things that might be creating barriers?

2. Do you have a clear sense, as Paul did, of the ministry God wants you to do?

3. Is your service to God characterized by humility as Paul's was? Make a list of some personal sacrifices your commitments have cost.

7
Empowered Citizens

Truth to Apply: As I open myself to God's power, I find great inner strength, and a new sense of Christ's deep love for me.

Key Verse: I pray that out of his glorious riches he may strengthen you with power though his Spirit in your inner being (Eph. 3:16).

Parents who forget to buy batteries can expect some forlorn young faces on Christmas morning. The toys are pretty, but just plain useless without the internal energy source to make them work. Unlike the toys in "The Nutcracker," they will never move without the addition of a separate energy source. Just for fun, think of some parallels between a battery's power and the characteristics of spiritual power. Share with others how you may have been "recharged" by the Lord at particular times of need in your spiritual journey.

The apostle Paul deeply understood that God's power energized his ministry to the Gentiles. He wrote in Romans 15:17-19 that all of his service to God had been accomplished through Christ. Everything he had said or done was through the power of the Holy Spirit. (The three Persons of the one God are so intertwined that when Paul writes of Christ's Spirit and the Holy Spirit he means the same power.) Paul reminds his Roman readers that the powerful display of signs and miracles that gave credence to his ministry came from God.

Earlier in Ephesians Paul taught that this power is the same power that raised Jesus from the dead. Every Christian has access to this "incomparably great power" (Eph. 1:19). Paul's first prayer recorded in this letter asks that the Ephesians would experience this power as one of the spiritual riches bequeathed to them. Since they had been chosen by God "to do good works" (Eph. 2:10) it was critical that they comprehend and use the boundless spiritual power available.

Our passage covers Paul's second prayer for the Ephesians. Here he describes God's power in greater detail, showing how it helps Christians begin to grasp the immensity of God's love. He wants all the members of the new community, the Church, to have breathless insight into the truly amazing abilities God's power gives them.

This prayer is for us as well. If by faith we claim this power, our service to God will also be totally "recharged"! Paul's prayer serves as an excellent model, showing prayer as the means of tapping God's power.

Light on the Text

Heartfelt Prayer (3:14, 15)

Paul resumes his intention to record his prayer for the Ephesians. He had begun chapter 3 with the words "for this reason," but then digressed to explain the mystery of the Church. Here he repeats the same words, "for this reason," continuing with "I kneel before the Father." What prompts the prayer? We need to look back to the end of chapter 2—the section Paul had just finished writing before his digression. There he had unfolded the truth that the citizens of Christ's Church are spiritually being built together to form a dwelling where God's Spirit lives. Thus, Paul is praying for a deepening of the faith of the Ephesians, to help them in experiencing this dwelling of God in their hearts.

A Jew did not necessarily kneel before God to pray. Jesus' Parable of the Publican and the Pharisee in Luke 18:11, 13 shows both men standing. No doubt deep emotion caused Paul to drop to his knees before God. During his tender farewell to the Ephesian elders Paul also knelt in prayer.

Paul kneels before "the Father." This term was more intimate than a Jew would normally use. But Paul had just taught in Ephesians 2:18 and 3:12 that Christ's reconciling work gives open access to God. Jesus' ministry of peace between persons and God gives believers the privilege to call God "Father." This was prophesied in the Old Testament. Paul quotes the II Samuel 7:14 reference in his second letter to the Corinthians: "I will be a Father to you, and you will be my sons and daughters, says the Lord Almighty."

Several other truths taught in Ephesians secure this new relationship. Paul called God "the Father of our Lord Jesus Christ" earlier in the letter. By virtue of our being united to Christ as His Body, members of the Church can call God Father. One of the spiritual blessings of the process of God's making us citizens of His new society is adoption into His family (Eph. 1:4). God is our Father and we, the Church, are members of His family. Paul says that His family members in Heaven and on earth have the right to call themselves His children because of this relationship. His family in Heaven consists of the believers who have died and now dwell with Him. The living Church below is His family on earth.

The Greek phrase in verse 1 is hard to translate. Some take it to mean "from whom *all fatherhood* derives its name." Paul may indeed have meant this as a secondary meaning. The preexisting reality of God as the Father is what patterned the earthly relationship of families. God was eternally Father to the Son. We do not make God a father figure by wish fulfillment, as Freud taught. Father figures (and fathers) exist because we have the Father in Heaven. This is even part of God's general revelation to humankind. Paul alluded to this in his speech on Mars' Hill to the members of the Areopagus. Some of their Greek poets sensed that there was one great God who created them, for they had written, "We are his offspring" (Acts 17:28, 29). God is doubly Father to believers: He fathered us in Creation and adopted us into His family at the new birth.

Paul's Prayer Requests (3:16-19)

3:16, 17a
Paul specifically prays for two things here: that the Ephesians will be strengthened with power in their inner beings through the Holy Spirit, and that Christ would dwell in their hearts through faith.

These two requests are linked because Christ's dwelling in their hearts was dependent upon the strengthening accomplished by the Father through the Holy Spirit's power. Both of the acts spring from God the Father's storehouse of spiritual riches. The trinitarian references here are impossible to miss. Each person in the Godhead plays a role in fortifying Christians. God the Father strengthens us using the Holy Spirit's power, which causes Christ to dwell in our hearts through faith.

The believers' inner beings and their hearts are synonymous expressions. In his first prayer Paul had prayed that the "eyes of their hearts" might be enlightened (Eph. 1:18). All these expressions refer to a person's soul, the part that communes with God. As God's power through His Spirit strengthens us, Christ dwells more completely within us. The sense of the verb "dwell" in the Greek means to "make one's abode." Christ comes to stay with us; He is not just a visitor passing through. The beautiful words from Revelation 3:20 apply here: "If anyone hears my voice and opens the door [of the heart], I will come in and eat with him, and he with me."

The famous commentator Matthew Henry described Christ's abiding with us this way: "Christ is always present with his people, by his gracious influences and operations. If the law of Christ be written in our hearts, and the love of Christ be shed abroad there, then Christ dwells there" *(Commentary on the Holy Bible)*.

The joy we experience from the dwelling of Christ in our hearts is a mere foretaste of the communion we'll experience in eternity. John describes the presentation of the bride of Christ to her Bridegroom in Revelation 21:2, 3: "I saw the Holy City, the new Jerusalem, coming down out of heaven from God, prepared as a bride beautifully dressed for her husband. And I heard a loud voice from the throne saying, 'Now the dwelling of God is with men, and he will live with them. They will be his people, and God himself will be with them and be their God.' " One of Christ's names prophesied of His first advent was "Immanuel" which means "God with us" (Isa. 7:14; Mt. 1:23). We experience this now; we will know it in its fullness in Heaven.

3:17b, 18 Paul makes three more petitions in these verses. He prays that they will be rooted and established in love; that they will have power to grasp the dimensions of Christ's love; and that, knowing this love, they will be filled with the fullness of God.

The verbs "rooted" and "established [grounded]" are horticultural and architectural terms, respectively. Christians are to have, as John Stott puts it, "deep roots and firm foundations." Love should be the preeminent feature of God's new community. God Himself is seen as believers express love one to another (I Jn. 4:12). When such love is shown, "God lives in us and his love is made complete in us." John and James both strongly teach that this love is not a sentimental emotion, but exhibits itself in self-sacrificing action.

Paul again prays for power to grasp the extent of Christ's love. He uses graphic spatial imagery to show its scope. Ancient commentators have noted that wide, long, high, and deep could be seen as the bars on the Cross. While this probably is not the direct image Paul was trying to convey, it is true that the Cross was the greatest demonstration of Christ's love for us.

57

Dimension	Application	Reference
Width	Indicates the breadth of peoples now included in the Church through Christ's reconciling work	(Eph. 2:12, 13)
Length	The eternal aspect of Christ's love	(Eph.1:4)
Depth	God's stooping down to our sinful condition in order to give us spiritual life through Christ	(Eph. 2:1-5)
Height	God's raising us up with Christ and seating us with Him in the heavenly realms	(Eph. 2:6)

3:19 Even though we can grasp some of this love, ultimately it surpasses knowledge. These dimensions shoot away from us in four directions—words just can't contain the whole of Christ's love for us. This is why we'll need an eternity to love God!

The result of knowing Christ's love is to be "filled to the measure of all the fullness of God." "Fullness" is one of the themes of Ephesians. It carries the meaning of perfection. God reckons us perfect by applying Christ's righteousnss to us, yet the whole of our Christian life involves a perfecting process. God the Refiner wants to purge the dross from us.

3:20, 21 God who is able to do "immeasurably more than all we ask or imagine." It is wonderful that God is not limited by the smallness of our prayers! God promises to accomplish this through us, by the power of the Spirit whom He has placed within us. God's mighty acts through His people, the Church, bring eternal glory to His name. God's limitless power is the Christian's and the Church's greatest resource.

For Discussion

1. Do you feel you need greater strengthening from God in your inner being? Share your thoughts with others. What promise can you claim?

2. What is the power at work within you? What are its limits? In what ways have you experienced God's power in your life?

3. What can you apply to your prayer life from the two prayers recorded in Ephesians?

8
United Citizens

Truth to Apply: I am called by God to promote unity among fellow Christians.

Key Verse: Make every effort to keep the unity of the Spirit through the bond of peace (Eph. 4:3).

Unity is a value humans seem to have instilled within them. Many organizations and institutions have been founded for the purpose of unity. For example, the League of Nations, and then later the United Nations, were organized to help the world's nations understand each other better and to serve as a tribunal for solving international problems. Labor unions bring workers together to gain leverage with employers on economic and safety concerns. The United States of America brought separate states and commonwealths under one government for mutual protection and political clout on the world scene. Sororities, fraternities, Kiwanis, The Junior League, etc., bring people together for friendship and community service.

God expects His Church to display the highest degree of unity. In your opinion, how is the Church doing in this area? What are some of its (past and present) successes? Failures?

Background/Overview: *Ephesians 4:1-8*

The first half of Ephesians, chapters 1—3, stresses the spiritual standing in Christ guaranteed to citizens of the Church. Paul has explained the doctrinal foundation of the Church members' heavenly blessings and privileges. Now beginning with chapter 4 he switches gears to make practical application of these doctrines. Paul brings us from the riches in the heavenly realms to the earthly plane, where Christ's Church members must pursue their daily lives. Since God created His Church to be "holy and blameless" and to display "the manifold wisdom of God," He requires high standards of His people.

The letter to the Ephesians was sent to the Christians in Ephesus and in other cities in Asia Minor to defend the integrity of Christian living amid the gross idolatry of pagan culture. The city of Ephesus was among the most important religious centers in all Asia Minor. It was a crossroads of communication, commerce, and craftsmanship—especially the trade of silversmithing and image making (Acts 19:23-28).

The cosmopolitan mood of Ephesus welcomed various philosophies and religions, most notably the cult of Diana, the Roman fertility goddess associated with the moon and hunting. Her temple at Ephesus was one of the seven wonders of the world. It was four times the size of the Parthenon at Athens. Worshipers of Diana believed that she, along with other gods, exerted influence over mankind and that life would be more pleasant and profitable if they pleased her. Sacrifices were made to her for that reason.

Paul opposed this cult vigorously on his third missionary journey. His defense—partly preserved in Ephesians—was a key reason for the spread of Christianity. Those believers, battling paganism and materialism in their worldly city, needed all the spiritual counsel Paul could give. We, too, live in a jaded, corrupt society. The truths of Ephesians still stand, offering strength and encouragement. Jesus Christ is still Lord of all. He alone still deserves our worship, love, and daily obedience. The Church has the great mission to shine forth God's light and to fight the forces of spiritual darkness. These final chapters of Ephesians outline God's strategy for His Church. The Bible passage in this lesson concerns the primary condition that must be met for spiritual effectiveness.

Light on the Text

Unity Among Believers (4:1-3)

Paul, writing from prison, urged those not in physical chains to be unified—united as tightly as possible according to the working of the Holy Spirit. He implored the Ephesians to walk worthy of their calling as Christians, and to stay united in belief and action. He pleaded strongly with them because unity was so vital to the growth of the Church.

4:1 Paul calls himself "a prisoner for the Lord" echoing the phrase "the prisoner of Christ Jesus" that he used in verse 3:1. He was a prisoner for the cause of Jesus Christ, and a prisoner of Caesar only because Christ allowed it for His greater purposes. Paul was willing to sacrifice his personal freedom for the Gospel. In so doing, he served as a model for the believers to whom he writes. In the rest of Ephesians, Paul often repeats the injunction to "live" their lives in accordance with God's high calling. Older versions use the word "walk" —which has a nice active ring to it. Note the repetition of the command in Ephesians 4:17; 5:2; 5:8; and 5:18.

Paul invokes his apostolic authority in the phrase "I urge you." God has so impressed on his heart the vision of a united Church that Paul begs his readers to live up to this ideal. Earlier in the letter he stressed the reality of the unity of the Church. This was the mystery that had so long been hidden.

Paul has used many images and phrases in earlier chapters to teach the organic unity of the Church. Here are some of them:

1. Christ's death has made "the two one" out of Jewish and Gentile believers. (2:14)

2. The dividing wall of hostility has been destroyed. (2:14)

3. "One new man" has been created out of Jews and Gentiles. (2:15)

4. Jews and Gentiles are reconciled to God as "one body." (2:16)

5. Gentiles are "fellow citizens" with Jewish believers. (2:19)

6. Jews and Gentiles are "members of God's household." (2:19)

7. Jews and Gentiles are being built together into one "holy temple in the Lord" where God dwells by His Spirit. (2:21, 22)

8. Gentiles are "heirs together with Israel." (3:6)

9. Gentiles are "members together of one body." (3:6)

10. Gentiles are "sharers together in the promise in Christ Jesus." (3:6)

4:2 Since the Church is truly one, God expects its members to show this oneness in their relationships. The calling they received was citizenship in God's new society. With citizenship comes the responsibility to cultivate new attitudes fostering unity. What four traits does Paul urge them to adopt? Humility, gentleness, patience, and forbearance ("bearing with one another in love"). Each of these is characterized by concern for another's well-being.

Older translations of Scripture use the word "lowliness" instead of "humility." True humility understands that we are lowly: creatures made by God and dependent on Him. We are created with "inbuilt deficits," needing most of all the help of God, and secondarily the help from other men and women.

The virgin Mary was not only thinking of her poor economic condition when she praised God for considering her "humble estate." She knew she had been blessed because of God's sovereign choice, not because of anything in her. Humility recognizes that we are not just finite, but sinners, too. Arrogance, the opposite, is scarcely appropriate when we have fallen so short of God's example of holiness.

Finally, humility keeps a goal in mind—the goal of unity. In Philippians 2:3, Paul urges "in humility consider others better than yourselves." He points to Christ as exemplifying humility. He "humbled (literally, "lowered") himself," setting aside the rights He has as God the Son and serving us by dying on a cross. The point is that to see our unity in Christ working out in practice, we must have that attitude of lowliness, setting aside our rights and being servants to others.

"Gentleness" (or "meekness") is often associated with lowliness and has a meaning close to it, focusing on our willingness to accept whatever befalls us as coming from God and useful to Him in making us Christlike. When we meet adversity or opposition with meekness, we do not struggle and grind against God but show a receptive heart at any changes He wants to bring to our character.

This does not mean we as Christians will refuse to eliminate injustice, even when it is directed against us. But we approach the unjust situation with a childlike receptivity to God, open to learn from Him even as we are reminding sinful, oppressive people of God's just character.

We need to see that neither humility nor gentleness equals spinelessness. But in a humble and gentle frame of mind we can turn to God in all circumstances, seeking opportunities to serve others even at the expense of what technically might be called our "rights." Only then will unity display itself among God's people.

The phrase, "be patient, bearing with one another in love," develops the point even further. Christians must bear with those who suffer physical, emotional, or other handicaps. We must accept one another, as we remember we all have shortcomings and need to grow up in Christ. Without such tolerance no group could function. Finally, we must show patience because God in Christ has shown patience and forgiveness toward us (Eph. 4:32).

4:3   Paul again stresses passionately that believers "Make every effort to keep the unity of the Spirit." The Church is unified by God's Spirit. The phrase "the bond of peace" refers to the peace bought by Christ's death. It is this peace with which His Spirit then fills the Church. But Christians can make it visible.

Oneness (4:4-6)

There are seven magnificent ways in which believers are one. These unities are based on the acts of the three Persons in the Godhead. The first three cluster around the Holy Spirit. He undergirds the reality of one Body by dwelling in every believer (Eph. 2:22). His indwelling is a deposit guaranteeing, or sealing, our one hope of redemption (Eph. 1:13, 14, 18).

The death and resurrection of the Lord Jesus Christ gives believers the basis for one faith and baptism. We look in faith to Christ's completed work on the cross for our salvation. Our baptism signifies that we have been buried and raised in Him (Eph. 2:6). Finally, the one God and Father of all gives unity because He is over all and through all and in all.

ONENESS THEMES

One Body	Rom. 12:5	form one body . . . each member belongs to all the others
One Spirit	I Cor. 12:13	baptized by one Spirit into one body . . . given the one Spirit to drink
One Hope of Your Calling	Rom. 8:23-25	wait eagerly for our adoption as sons . . . in this hope we were saved
One Lord	I Cor. 8:6	one Lord, Jesus Christ, through whom all things came and through whom we live
One Faith	Heb. 12:2	Jesus, the author and perfecter of our faith
One Baptism	Gal. 3:27	baptized into Christ
One God and Father of all	I Cor. 8:6	one God, the Father, from whom all things came and for whom we live

Gift of Grace (4:7-10)

Christ has given each of us grace so we can faithfully fill our separate roles as members of His Body. Paul quotes Psalm 68:18 to explain how Christ's exaltation enabled Him to give spiritual gifts to His followers. The image is of a conqueror distributing spoils. Christ's death and resurrection has made Him conqueror "far above all rule and authority, power and dominion" (Eph. 1:21). Now He shares the gain with His Church. Christ's ascension on high could only follow His willingness to descend to earth where the victory over sin was accomplished. God honored Christ for this sacrifice by seating Him at His right hand in the heavenly realms. Ephesians 1:22 says "God placed all things under his feet and appointed him to be head over everything for the Church." In His exaltation Christ fills the whole universe.

Philippians 2 is a parallel passage stressing Christ's willingness to let go of His heavenly privilege to accept a debasing death on an earthly cross. Because of this, "God exalted him to the highest place and gave him the name that is above every name."

In the next chapter we will learn how the gifts Christ gives to His Church help it grow to spiritual maturity.

For Discussion

1. What steps could you take to live a life more worthy of your calling?

2. How can you reflect the unity of the Holy Spirit in your relationships with others?

3. Does your church encourage each person to use the grace he or she has been given? If so, give an example of how it is working.

9
Growing Citizens

Truth to Apply: As an individual member, using the gifts Christ has given me, I can help the Church grow into maturity.

Key Verse: From him the whole body, joined and held together by every supporting ligament, grows and builds itself up in love, as each part does its work (Eph. 4:16).

In the book *Fearfully and Wonderfully Made,* Dr. Paul Brand reflects on the nature of cancer cells. The cells, once normal, suddenly cease to function interdependently with other cells. Multiplying wildly, the cancer cells drive out the good cells, stealing life from them.

Brand sees parallels between this phenomenon and life within Christ's Body, the Church. What similarities does this suggest to you? What is the "cure"?

Background/Overview: *Ephesians 4:11-16*

In the letter to the Ephesians Paul exhorts his readers to live lives worthy of the new nature that was given them in Christ Jesus. He emphasizes the eternal purpose of God to save men and women through faith in Jesus Christ, then clearly presents the natural outgrowth of such behavior. Since Christ's death broke down the wall of hostility between Jew and Gentile, all Christians are called to a new kind of life: one that moves in the direction of Christian maturity.

How can Christians grow without it becoming a ritualistic duty? First, God makes Himself known to us. Ephesians 1 stresses that God's long-term purpose was to reveal Himself.

Second, He has redeemed us at great cost, turning aside His wrath by Christ's blood and offering peace to those who believe. As Ephesians 2 sums up, believers have been made alive in Christ. Only on the basis of God's redemption does He then call us to service.

The Christian life is not a moralistic duty. God not only calls us to holiness, but also, through regeneration, draws out our hearts to desire it, and through the indwelling of the Spirit gives us the necessary power.

Ephesians 4:11-16 takes a look at how God intended His Church to function. We see how the gifts Christ gives His Church are meant to involve all Christians. Paul reminds us that the Church is a single Body, with Christ as its head. All members are obliged to grow up into the Head and to build up other members.

Christ carefully gifted His Church to assure the healthy growth of His Body. Paul tells us the marks of a mature Church, and how each member builds it up.

Light on the Text

The Role of Leaders (4:11, 12)

We saw in the last lesson that Christ apportioned grace to every member of the Church. Leaders have been given specific gifts for the express purpose of preparing "God's people for works of service." The all-too-common situation of a ministerial staff doing the bulk of the church work (while the congregation does little more than pay the bills and watch) is a travesty of God's intention.

The four kinds of leaders Christ raised up to establish His Church were: apostles, prophets, evangelists, pastors/teachers. In I Corinthians 12:28 and here, apostles are listed first. This is because their particular job was to push back the frontier and establish new churches where people had not heard the Gospel. God gave them a unique authority for leadership in that they filled the role of His spokesmen. Many of them were granted the privilege, by the Holy Spirit, of writing the New Testament Scriptures. Ephesians 2:19 states that the Church is built on the foundation of the apostles and prophets, which presumably includes their writings. Because the apostles were eyewitnesses of the risen Christ, they had the unique mission of recording their testimony. Theirs was a foundational ministry to the Church today. Being a literal eyewitness of the risen Christ was part of their credentials (Acts 1:22).

Prophets, too, in the sense of foretelling the future and speaking new revelations from God, had a foundational gift that the early church needed. The New Testament Scriptures were still being written, so the Holy Spirit communicated through such chosen spokespersons as Agabus (Acts 11:28; 21:10) and Philip's four daughters (Acts 21:9). (Denominations that believe this gift continues into our age will normally uplift the primacy of Scripture by testing a prophecy against the truths in God's Word.)

One aspect of the gift of prophecy—edification—is still much needed by the Church. In I Corinthians 14:1-3 Paul says to desire the gift of prophecy because the one who prophesies "speaks to men for their strengthening, encouragement and comfort." All who faithfully proclaim God's Word today are prophets in this sense.

The third group Paul mentions are evangelists. They were people who did not stay in any one place but traveled widely preaching the Gospel in order to win others to personal faith in the atoning work of Christ.

Philip, who preached to the Ethiopian eunuch, is called an evangelist (Acts 21:8). Evangelists boldly enter new territory to share God's Word with the unconverted. Pioneering missionaries are certainly evangelists.

The last group, pastor/teachers, appears to be one kind of leader with the twin gifts of shepherding God's people and speaking forth His Word to them. The gift of teaching can exist without the gift of pastoring. Nevertheless, all pastors, to shepherd properly, need to be able to effectively communicate God's Word to their flock. Unlike the apostles or most evangelists, pastor/teachers are called to one location to help build up that particular church.

The Role of Lay People (4:12, 13)

The role of leaders is to prepare God's people for works of service. Toward what goal do we serve as we become prepared? The goal of edifying, or building up, the rest of the Body of Christ. A pastor/teacher explains love as Paul describes it in I Corinthians 13, for example. We hear him, and our minds are given a sensitive humility that aids us in seeing our own gift—perhaps the gift of showing mercy (Rom. 12:8), a special kind of mercifulness, so that we may find ourselves particularly able to visit the sick, encouraging them in Christ.

All of these gifts are bestowed for one purpose—that the saints might be coordinated for the work of serving in Christ's name. Each person's gift is to be used as a contribution to the others.

Obviously, there is no place in this scheme of things for comparing gifts, or for ranking one above the other. All the gifts are important, and each must be functioning for a church to be truly balanced in its ministry.

The lists of gifts in Scripture are probably not exhaustive. The Holy Spirit can develop abilities within us that we couldn't dream we had!

What specific needs does your local church have? Write these in the left-hand column of the chart on the next page. Link the need with the gifts that would apply. Try to respond to a specific need first, for that is how God reveals a person's gift or gifts.

Needs	Gifts
1	Teaching
2	Mercy
3	Helps
4	Administration
5	Wisdom
6	Knowledge
7	Evangelism
8	Serving
9	Encouraging
10	Giving
11	Prophesying
12	

Others:

What will happen when we accept the New Testament teaching and begin exercising our own gifts? Paul tells us in verse 13 that we will "reach unity in the faith." The reference here is not so much to the individual Christian as to the church as a unit. Of course, no church can grow as a unit without growing in its parts. But Paul's burden at this point was that the Church would grow up in oneness with each member contributing to the whole. If the Church is to do the work of reconciliation it must preserve its unity. No church can win outsiders if it is all divided up inside.

As the Church grows in maturity it reaches "to the whole measure of the fullness of Christ." This means reaching the goal set for it. The Church is the incarnation of the ascended Christ and, therefore, is called upon to be completely molded in His image. God has made "one new man" out of Jew and Gentile. He expects this "man," the Body of Christ, to reach mature adulthood. Nothing distresses a parent more than for a child to fail to attain physical or mental maturity. So, too, with our Heavenly Father.

73

Marks of Growth (4:14-16)

The adult should be able to make up his or her mind and stick to it. Yet, some are like rudderless boats tossed about on a sea of differing philosophies and contradicting ideas.

There were false teachers within the early church whose prime purpose was to lure astray the immature Christians. The apostle warns the Ephesians against allowing such teachings to misguide them.

In spite of all that false teachers might do, true believers are warned here to remain faithful to the truth delivered to them and to do it with love in their hearts. The first defense against spiritual attack is truth, as Paul will stress later in Ephesians 6:14. Truth is the primary guard against falsehood in teaching or conduct. We are to speak it to help others—but in love, that its cutting edge may ultimately heal.

The entire Body, if it is whole and growing properly, receives its direction from Christ, its head. Each member of the Body contributes to every other part so that the Body functions in an orderly manner. No matter how insignificant any member of the Body may seem to be, that person has a real contribution to make. Paul teaches that growth takes place through difference, not sameness. No two parts do the same thing. Love is the element holding the whole Body together. This love grows as individual members do the work to which they are called. Each member, therefore, has a very real influence on the health of the entire Body.

For Discussion

1. What would you say to a person who claims, "I don't need to go to church. People just get in the way of my vision of God. I can worship better by just going alone into the woods with my Bible"?

2. How can this Ephesian passage speak to our society's current fascination with astrology and reincarnation?

3. Do you always speak forth the truth in love? What are the things that sometimes hinder you?

10
Self-controlled Citizens

Truth to Apply: I am called to increase self-control in my life in order to better imitate God.

Key Verse: Put on the new self, created to be like God in true righteousness and holiness (Eph. 4:24).

Celebrities on TV talk shows confess their addictions to drugs or alcohol. Tabloids hint at illicit sexual liaisons among the stars. High rollers at casinos sometimes hock the car they came in to keep playing the tables.

Like pagan Ephesus, our post-Christian society is "without hope and without God in the world" (Eph. 2:12). The havoc found all over the world rises out of a hellish emptiness that people cannot face. People are frantically trying to find fulfillment in things that cannot bring it. They use drugs or alcohol, but end up in worse shape than before. They experiment with pre- and extra-marital sex and find it dehumanizing. They buy luxurious gadgets, but these prove unsatisfying. Is there any stopping this mad, out-of-control search for meaning? Why is our age so addicted?

Paul's readers consisted mainly of Gentiles, who lived in a pagan society without the moral standards of God's Law. As Acts 19:1-20 reveals, Paul faced demonic opposition while he ministered in Ephesus. Many of those who became Christians had practiced wicked deeds, including sorcery. Moreover, idolatry had a strong hold on western Asia Minor through the temple of Artemis, or Diana. Because the message of Christ called for a repudiation of idolatry and the immoral practices idolatry promoted, the silversmiths and other tradespeople tried to stamp out the Christian preachers.

Paul talks about the old life of paganism, the pattern of living characteristic of the Gentiles. He is aware that some people in the Ephesian fellowship have not all changed their ways. This is not to be so among Christians. The world should recognize the difference in us by the way we act. If there is no change, it shows there is no real understanding of what is meant by being Christian.

Paul had several sources for his moral advice. The described conduct went back to the teaching of Jesus, or was forged out of distinctly Christian principles. Other moral and ethical injunctions were part of the Jewish teaching still recognized as valid for Christians. Yet others were the common property of the Greco-Roman civilization, given them by God's general revelation (see Rom. 2:15). Through the Holy Spirit's guidance Paul draws on these strands to present a more complete code of behavior for the citizens of God's new community.

Light on the Text

Pagan Depravity (4:17, 19)

Sometimes when we write to people, we try to tell them what they should not do. In this Scripture Paul gives a capsule description of the pagan way of life, the life apart from Christ—what a Christian is not to be.

Unity is the theme in the first part of the fourth chapter. Paul describes the mature person: "until we all reach unity in the faith and in the knowledge of the Son of God and become mature, attaining to the whole measure of the fullness of Christ" (Eph. 4:13). Here in this latter section of the same chapter Paul presents us with a sober and straightforward look at human beings who do not have God's Spirit.

Living "in the futility of their thinking" is characteristic of those without God. Marked by emptiness, frustration, and delusion, the godless live out a life of hopelessness and slavery to the whims of the flesh. They are "separated from the life of God" because of their "darkened" understanding, their "ignorance," and the "hardening of their hearts."

The unbelievers' understanding is darkened, not comprehending the truth of God. They are separated from God due to their willful ignorance. Romans 1 teaches that people consciously repress the knowledge of God. People know they will have to change their life-style if they yield to God. Paul, as a missionary to the Gentiles, was dedicated to helping them see the folly of their way and the more excellent life offered them in Jesus Christ.

The apostle describes the pagan life as being like a petrified heart. The term "having lost all sensitivity" suggests a callus, like that which forms around a bone break. It eventually becomes harder than the bone itself. The pagan unbeliever is insensitive because his or her conscience has become calloused.

In addition to callousness, the pagan way is characterized as a life of abandonment to all kinds of unclean, immoral practices. It is as if Paul suggests a kind of animal existence in which the unbelieving person acts like a beast, with no shame, totally mastered by self-serving desires. One has only to read the personals in certain magazines, or walk past the X-rated movie marquees, to see this same depravity at work.

Bright, New Clothes (4:20-24)

Paul reminds his readers that they did not come to know Christ this way. When God saved them He immediately lifted them from the muck of their lives to be seated in the heavenly realms with Christ (see Eph. 2:3-6). Because of the new faith instilled within them it was inconceivable that they would cling to their past depraved ways.

Proper indoctrination in the Gospel of Christ should impress us with the necessity of cleaning up our lives, learning to live by Christian discipline, and refraining from participation in the hardened, insensitive, sensual life-style of the unbelieving world. When people have "heard" Christ and have been "taught in him," they have access to the "truth" in Him. This truth brings about change.

The key to Paul's message of change is found in his image of comparing the old self to a soiled garment. Christians are to take it off and discard it forever! As long as they continue to wrap their old ways around themselves, they will remain dirty, foul, and unable to know a "clean bill of health." Paul says, in essence, "Take off those old dirty clothes that identify you as a member of a dirty, immoral, and calloused life-style."

No person can remain spiritually naked. He or she must "put on" as well as "take off." The work is not complete until there has been a complete change of clothes, a new kind of adornment for a cleaned-up spirit. The fleshly existence of a person should reflect the condition of that person's spirit. Isaiah 61:10 uses the same imagery: "I delight greatly in the Lord; my soul rejoices in my God. For he has clothed me with garments of salvation and arrayed me in a robe of righteousness, as a bridegroom adorns his head like a priest, and as a bride adorns herself with her jewels."

Notice that change takes place by the process of being "made new in the attitude of your minds." Renewal doesn't come simply from following a new set of rules or joining a new group. It moves from the inside out. Genuine transformation comes as a result of a transformation within. The new self is created to be like God in "true righteousness and holiness." Ephesians 1:4 assures us that we were chosen by God to be holy and blameless in His sight. Here we see that He makes us so by giving us a new self to put on. The joyful banner cry of the Christian is this: "If anyone is in Christ, he is a new creation; the old has gone, the new has come!" (II Cor. 5:17).

Code of Conduct (4:25-32)

4:25   The Pauline concept of the Church as the Body of Christ comes through here when he speaks of being members with one another. If this kind of reciprocal relationship exists among Christians, then lying cannot be allowed. It would be the same as if the senses and nerves of the physical body passed false messages to the brain. The body would be crippled and probably die.

4:26   Anger is one of the normal, human emotions. But it must be used constructively or it can do great damage. Anger rising within us warns us that we need to straighten out a problem with the other person. When we peacefully seek to do so we can experience anger and yet not sin.

Selfish, unleashed anger hurts both the subject and the object. While we need to be angry with sin, we must be cautious about being angry with people. Jesus, in the Sermon on the Mount (Mt. 5:21-26), insists that anger is the root of murder. Therefore, one must cut the root at once before it has a chance to grow and bear its bitter fruit. Scripture commands, "Do not let the sun go down while you are still angry."

4:27   Stewing in our anger gives Satan a foothold, as does holding on to any other sinful practice. Our enemy, who never sleeps, is always alert to every opportunity to mess up our lives. Therefore, we need to keep careful watch of our attitudes and actions.

4:28   Paul's admonition to the thief is an eye-opener. It makes us realize again that the early church contained all kinds of people. The church had welcomed into her fellowship those who had made a livelihood by stealing. Paul wants this new Christian to be changed in two ways: to learn to work "with his own hands," and to "share with those in need." A life of working and giving would indeed be an indication that a thief had been changed by the new life in Christ!

4:29   Does anyone need to tell us that the tongue causes more trouble than anything else? James says the tongue "is set on fire by hell" (Jas. 3:6). The unwholesome talk Paul warns against includes gossip, slander, profanity, lying, and idle words. None of these things should be given a place in the believer's life. Every word should have the purpose of building up the community of faith rather than tearing it down. Our tongues can either minister to others or grievously hurt them.

4:30   We hurt the Spirit when we disobey Him, just as a child hurts parents by disobedience. The "seal" is God's stamp of ownership placed upon us when we believe in Christ as Savior. "The day of redemption" speaks of the whole process from the moment we are saved until the moment Christians are glorified in Heaven.

4:31,   The two verses list opposite traits that show the drastic
32   change new life in Christ should bring. The negative traits to be gotten rid of are: bitterness, rage and harmful anger, brawling and slander, and every form of malice. These evil actions usually grow from one another. Bitterness comes from brooding over an injury. Rage is the burst of temper that follows anger. Anger grows from the pent-up bitterness. Brawling and slander mark the all-out fight unchecked rage can spark!

The positive traits to adopt are kindness, compassion, and forgiveness. The law of life that ought to rule in Christian circles is this: we are to treat one another as Christ treats us. As He forgives us, so are we to forgive others. As He speaks softly to us, so are we to speak to others. As He loves us, in the same manner we are to love all the household of faith. By this change in our total behavior, the nonbeliever will sense something has happened to us that has transformed us inside out.

A Life of Love (5:1, 2)

The new creature is a follower of God with all the sincerity and openness of "dearly loved children." Our supreme example of this new way of living is Christ, who loved us so much that He gave Himself for us as "a fragrant offering and sacrifice to God." The Old Testament burnt offerings gave an aroma pleasing to the

80

Lord (Lev. 1:9). Those continual sacrifices foreshadowed Christ's one great, acceptable sacrifice.

Christ's model of love teaches us how to love. As we follow Christ's example we become "imitators of God." To imitate God means to seek to be like Him. But is this possible? Yes, for three reasons: 1) we are created in the image of God; 2) the Holy Spirit, the Enabler, dwells within us; and 3) by regenerating grace we have become God's children.

IMITATORS OF GOD

1. Mt. 5:48	"Be perfect, therefore, as your heavenly Father is perfect."
2. I Jn. 4:11	"Since God so loved us, we also ought to love one another."
3. Jn. 15:12	"My command is this: Love each other as I have loved you."
4. Rom. 15:2, 3	"Each of us should please his neighbor for his good, to build him up. For even Christ did not please himself."
5. II Cor. 8:7, 9	"Excel in this grace of giving. Our Lord Jesus Christ . . . for your sakes became poor, so that you through his poverty might become rich."

For Discussion

1. Is your tongue a problem? What resources do you have to help control it?

2. How can you avoid grieving the Holy Spirit?

3. What is your experience with practicing forgiveness? Do you consistently extend forgiveness in your relationships with other Christians?

11
Pure Citizens

Truth to Apply: As a "child of light," I am called to a high standard of sexual purity.

Key Verse: But among you there must not be even a hint of sexual immorality, or of any kind of impurity, or of greed, because these are improper for God's holy people (Eph. 5:3).

The apostle Paul uses light as a metaphor for holiness. Consider the physical qualities of light in order to grasp the many layers of this image. How does light promote purity or wholeness? There are a number of ways:

1. Housekeeping: light reveals where the dirt is, so thorough cleaning may be done.

2. Surgery: a laser instrument probes and cuts away diseased portions of the body, promoting healing and wholeness.

3. Jewel cutting: a jeweler's lamp reveals the minute flaws in a stone, which he then cuts away to have a perfect gem.

4. Healing: sunlight or ultraviolet light cures many skin or vitamin-deficiency diseases.

5. Bleaching: strong light fades stains, thus improving the fabric's appearance.

Throughout Scripture, light represents God's holiness and glory. Our passage applies the metaphor to us, spotlighting our call to purity. This call has internal and external aspects. We are to be light—lamps reflecting God's holiness—but we are also to be searchlights, scouring the darkness to expose society's sins. Does this seem like a formidable challenge for you? In what specific ways?

Background/Overview: *Ephesians 5:3-20*

Paul has already introduced the image of darkness in the previous passage to describe the "darkened" understanding of the Gentiles' sinful life-styles. Gross sexual impurity characterized much of pagan Gentile life because of the perverse mystery religions. Artemis (also called Diana), whom Ephesus glorified with the slogan "Great is Artemis of the Ephesians" (Acts 19:28), was a fertility goddess. (Her images always show her as multibreasted.) Cult prostitution was integral to her worship.

Heretical Gnostic-like teaching was also taking root in Ephesus. Influenced by Greek thought, and fully blossomed in the second century A.D., Gnosticism taught that the body was an evil prison house from which the soul should seek escape. Since only the soul counted, some Gnostics taught that it didn't matter what one did with one's body. They thus indulged in unrestrained sexual activity. They were "pearls," they claimed, who could not be stained by any outward mud. One later Gnostic teacher, Epiphanes, taught that promiscuity was God's law. Homosexuality so permeated Greek social structure that family life had disintegrated. Since such thought and behavior blanketed Ephesus, Paul strongly warns his readers that God's community, the Church, must have absolutely no hint of immorality tainting its life. Rather, it must shine forth as light in such darkness.

Light on the Text

Sex Idols (5:3-7)

It's ironic that movie stars and rock musicians are often hailed as idols or "sex goddesses." Our society may not worship a meteorite that fell from the sky (which the Ephesian image of Diana was), but those with meteoric film or music careers are accorded similar devotion. Scripture calls sexual obsession idolatry and minces no words—no one who pursues such a life-style can expect to have "any inheritance in the kingdom of Christ and of God." It is because "of such things God's wrath comes on those who are disobedient." These are sober words against serious offenses in God's eyes.

5:3, 4   Paul describes six kinds of sexual sin that greatly displease God. When Scripture goes into this kind of detail, we had better listen. Immorality and impurity cover the whole gamut of outward sexual practice: fornication, adultery, cult sexual practices (which some Gnostics drew into their "Christian" rituals), homosexuality. Scripture calls this "greed" because such life-styles are insatiable, always coveting more. Verse 4 deals with "dirty words from dirty minds" as John Stott describes them: obscenity, foolish talk, coarse joking. This kind of behavior treats others as mere objects of lust, rather than building each other up in love.

These actions, thoughts, and words are "improper" and "out of place" for God's holy people, Paul stresses. God has rescued His people from such "cravings" of their sinful natures (Eph. 2:3), giving them life and lifting them to spiritual heights. Moreover, God's own Spirit dwells within each of them as a seal of the redeeming work He is doing within (Eph. 1:13).

In his first letter to the Corinthians (whose city was also vice-ridden), Paul insists that our union with the Holy Spirit precludes any sinful sexual dalliances. How could we, who are part of the very Body of Christ, even think of linking up our bodies with prostitutes (I Cor. 6:15, 16)? Our God is a jealous lover; Christ's bride must be pure.

Sexual sins are so devastating because they are sins against one's very being. Our sexuality is an intrinsic part of who we are, but it can be degraded to a pursuit of mere physical gratification alone. This is why immorality can bring such great emptiness.

5:5, 6   Unrestrained sexual sin is surely idolatry. Such a person worships the god, Sex, rather than the true God, and thus has no hope of a heavenly inheritance. Paul warns his Ephesian readers not to let anyone "deceive [them] with empty words" about these things: God's wrath is coming on the disobedient who indulge in such a pattern of life. Christians, therefore, are not to be partners with such people.

Light in the Lord (5:8-13)

5:8 The Asian Christians were once "darkness" but are now
"light" in the Lord. The metaphors refer to our spiritual
being. The "old self" was dead, darkness, without hope;
the "new self" is alive, light, with access to God by His
Spirit. Life and light are inextricably linked. God's light
gives us spiritual life. By virtue of our union with Christ,
we, too, become light and are to live as children of light.
Jesus taught that He was the light of the world and that,
by extension, His followers are the light of the world.
God has given the Church the awesome responsibility of
standing in as Christ's representatives to the world. In
the address to the Ephesian church in Revelation 2:5
God likens their position of influence to a "lampstand."

5:9 When Christians live as children of light, what is the
fruit of the light? Paul says it consists in all goodness,
righteousness, and truth. These traits are a blessed
contrast to the awful litany of sexual sins just listed. The
phrase "fruit of the light" is reminiscent of the phrase
"fruit of the Spirit" in Galatians 5:22. There the crop
includes love, joy, peace, patience, kindness, goodness,
faithfulness, gentleness, and self-control. Most of these
attributes Paul discussed in Ephesians 4.

5:10 Not only must Christians exhibit the fruit of the Holy
Spirit; they must "find out what pleases the Lord." God
has recorded in His holy Word what pleases Him. Only
by reading and meditating on it faithfully can we expect
to find out what pleases God. Of course, God not only
wants us to know what pleases Him, but to live
accordingly. As James says, "Anyone who listens to the
word but does not do what it says is like a man who
looks at his face in a mirror and, after looking at himself,
goes away and immediately forgets what he looks like.
But the man who looks intently into the perfect law that
gives freedom, and continues to do this, not forgetting
what he has heard, but doing it—he will be blessed in
what he does" (Jas. 1:23-25).

5:11 Paul again repeats the command to have nothing to do
with the sins of disobedient people, termed here

"fruitless deeds of darkness." "Fruitless," of course, contrasts to the fruit of the Spirit in a Christian's life. The word "fruitless" brings to mind Christ's warnings that branches which bear no fruit will be gathered up and burned. He will judge the fruitlessness of both Christians and non-Christians. Rather than being attracted to deeds of darkness, Christians, as the Lord's light, are to expose them.

5:12-14 Paul didn't describe the particulars of the pagans' sexual sin because it was too shameful. We should emulate Paul here and avoid prurient interest in our society's sins. As we live our lives as "light in the Lord," the contrast should be dramatic enough to shame sinners. As Christ's light shines forth from us, the sins will not only be exposed in the sense of naked revelation, but the sinner will see the sin for what it is. After all, it was Christ's life-giving light that initially shined on all who have come to Him. Paul is probably citing a portion of a baptismal chant when he quotes: "Wake up, O sleeper, rise from the dead, and Christ will shine on you."

Wise Lives (5:15-20)

Paul warns again, "Be very careful, then, how you live." We are to live not as unwise people, but as wise. ("Live" is a theme word in this letter, rendered "walk" in the KJV.) The concept of spiritual wisdom always refers to knowledge of God and obedience to His will.

Proverbs presents the wise man as one walking in the ways of the Lord. Verse 17 contrasts foolishness with understanding what the Lord's will is. Since the days are evil, we are to make the most of every opportunity. Instead of being caught up in the sterile cycle of self-gratification, Christians are to "buy up" every chance to please God. Christians who accomplish great things for God have a keen sense of their mission (what needs to be done since the days are evil) and of time (which they make the most of).

5:17-20 Wise believers avoid the folly of the world, seeking instead God's will. One practice Paul commands is to avoid drunken debauchery. Instead, be filled with the

Spirit! Drunkenness invoked the spirit of the god Bacchus for pagan Greeks. But Spirit-filled Christians are flooded with such joy and thankfulness that they cannot cease singing! Their worship and conversation with each other draws on the Psalms and other musical compositions. Believers' hearts well up with musical praise as the Spirit reminds them of all God has done for them. A thankful spirit characterizes believers who have the Holy Spirit filling their lives. This praise worships the Triune God: by the Holy Spirit, giving thanks to the Father, in the name of the Lord Jesus Christ. God's people are not only light, but they also have a God-given lightness in their hearts.

For Discussion

1. Has your sensitivity to God's sexual standards been blunted by the culture? What steps can you take to correct this?

2. How are you reflecting God's light in practical ways?

3. Do you have music in your heart from God's Spirit? What does it "sound" like?

12
Relating Citizens

Truth to Apply: Membership in God's new community affects how I behave in my family and work relationships.

Key Verse: Submit to one another out of reverence for Christ (Eph. 5:21).

Whether it's husbands and wives, children and parents, or work colleagues—when different wills are in close contact, there is bound to be some confict. You might call it a natural law. Conflicting ideas and wills are normal in our human situation. Because everyone wants help in their relationships there are countless best-selling books, seminars, newspaper columns, and magazine articles on the subject.

People handle conflict in many different ways. For example:

1. Eliminate one of the conflicting parties (as in divorce or firing).

2."Clam up" and refuse to deal with the conflict.

3. Resolve the differences of opinion so that a consensus can be reached.

4. Decide to compromise.

5. Give in to the desires of another or to the wishes of a group.

These different ways are neither mutually exclusive nor equally desirable; they often overlap when applied to a concrete situation. As you look into your past performance with conflict management, how would you describe your "style"?

The theme of the Letter to the Ephesians is unity. Into a disordered world where sin has produced the fragmentation of personal lives and the alienation of nations, the Gospel comes as the power to heal and unify. The source of that power is in the Person of Jesus Christ, who has won redemption for us (Eph. 1:7) and unity for the universe (1:10). His authority rests in His supreme exaltation (1:20-23).

We, in our turn, are called to live out that unity as citizens of God's community. As we have seen in chapters 4 and 5, Paul has given many commands to individual Christians. Now we enter the section of commands to social units—Christians in a family and Christians at work. As the oneness of Christ's Body is realized, and the Church grows up into Christ, its head, the redeemed life of unity will be reflected in all these relationships.

It is important to realize how revolutionary Paul's words were to the Asian believers. Family life in that culture was in a sorry state. Greek and Roman influences had deeply distorted God's order. Greek wives existed primarily to provide legitimate offspring to their husbands, who sought companionship elsewhere. The Roman law of *Patris Potestas* put women totally under the control of their fathers and then their husbands. This authority was so complete that a man could command death for anyone in his household: wife, child, or slave. Roman law gave slaves no legal rights, considering them their masters' property. The mutual love and respect Paul requires was something new indeed!

Light on the Text

The Key to Right Relationships (5:21-32)

5:21 Paul's counsel to mutual submission does not come in a vacuum. It has a firm foundation, theologically and practically. First of all, Paul is not talking to raw recruits off the street. He is talking to members of the Body of Christ (though not perfect by any means). All that he has to say presupposes the renewal of life in Christ and the consequent renewal of the hope for a real human community.

In the previous passage Paul commanded us to be filled with the Holy Spirit, who will then cause our conversation with one another to have joyful song underlying it. This next verse commands us to demonstrate our respect for Christ by putting each other first. Paul uses the word "submit" 23 times in his letters. The Son is our model for submission. The Gospels teach that He always submitted His will to the Father's. (His prayer in the Garden of Gethsemane shows what a struggle it could be.) In I Corinthians 15:28 it says that when God finally puts everything under Christ, then the Son will be made subject to the Father, so that God may be all in all. Mutual submission, the teaching of this verse, is the opposite of self-centeredness. The relationships in God's community are based on the redeemed lives of its members.

5:22 The word "submit" does not appear in verse 22 in the earliest Greek texts. Literally verses 21 and 22 read, "submitting yourselves one to another in the fear of Christ: wives, unto your own husbands, as unto the Lord."

The phrase "as unto the Lord," does not mean that husbands have authority equal to Christ's, but rather that a wife submits voluntarily to her husband out of her reverence for Christ. There is much resistance today to the word "submission" because it is misunderstood to imply an unequal power relationship. Jesus is not one who dominates His people, but one who has sacrificed everything to give them life, growth, and health. Christ is our Lord, but He uses His authority and headship to sustain us.

5:23, 24 Wives should understand that the husband's headship in the marriage, which is a "one body" relationship (Gen. 2:24), should emulate Christ's role as Head in His union with His Body, the Church. The Church submits to

Christ by growing and building itself up in love. Each member, by the power of the Holy Spirit, seeks to have his or her life manifest spiritual fruit: kindness, compassion, forgiveness. In the same way, the wife must willingly submit to her husband and strive to exhibit these traits in the marriage relationship. This is only right, for a Christian wife's submission to her husband comes in the context of the mutual submission that one believer offers to another.

The phrase "in everything" means that the wife must not selfishly hold back any part of herself. It doesn't mean that the husband can make any demand he wishes. "Out of reverence for Christ" is the overarching canopy for all marital actions. The intent of the word "submit" for the wife is self-giving love rather than blind obedience.

Total subjection had been the social condition of Paul's married female readers. Here he respectfully addresses them as equal members of the Body of Christ. In essence, Paul says that the way to have a happy marriage is to willingly put your husband's desires first. He will give the exact same principle to the husbands in the next verses. The old cliché about the way to have a good marriage seems appropriate here: each partner should give 100% (rather than 50/50).

5:25-31 Perhaps more verses are addressed to the husbands because the society gave them so much opportunity to abuse their leadership responsibilities. Rather than dictatorially reigning over their households, they are to love their wives. This is not an unspecified, sentimental sort of love, but it is to be exercised in a manner "just as Christ loved the Church." The pattern wives look to is the response of the Church to Christ as head. But the pattern husbands look to is staggering: it is nothing less than the love Christ displays for the Church!

How did Christ show His great love for his Bride, the Church? By giving Himself up for her. Christ gave up His heavenly glory and humbled Himself by becoming human. He also showed His great love by yielding to the ignominious death on a cross for our sins. No sacrifice a husband could make for his wife can approach the depth of Christ's love. Yet he is called to love his wife in this same manner. The husband's love for his wife is to be as unconditional as was Christ's for His Church.

5:26, 27	Christ's purpose in dying for the Church was to make her holy. The image of cleansing the bride with water may be an allusion to the ceremonial bridal bath that was a wedding custom of that culture. It surely also refers to baptism in connection with our spiritual cleansing by the water of God's Word. Christ's sanctifying work in His Church will make her radiant for the heavenly nuptial feast (Rev. 19:7, 8; 21:2). As we, the Church, stand with our Bridegroom for the marriage supper of the Lamb, we will at last be "holy and blameless"!

5:28, 29	The headship of the husband consists in loving and giving himself as Christ gave Himself for the Church. And Paul, on the basis of the "one flesh" doctrine in Creation, argues the reasonableness of that love. In loving his wife, the man is actually loving himself. Marriage so fuses a husband and wife that the nourishing care a person gives the other partner is lavished on his or her own body. Just as Christ feeds and cares for his Body, the Church, so should a Christian husband show loving concern for his wife.

A Profound Mystery (5:31-33)

In God's eyes marriage mystically binds the partners into "one flesh." His goal at Creation for marriage was the total union of two people: emotionally, spiritually, physically. (How appropriate that the physical union of two people can bring forth the "one flesh" of a child.) Earthly marriage can only dimly mirror the profound mystery of the union between Christ and His Church. That Christian marriage does show forth this spiritual reality, however, should give believers sober pause.

Children and Parents (6:1-4)

6:1	Disobedience to parents is a serious sin in Scripture (see Rom. 1:29-31 and II Tim. 3:1-5). Spoiled children lead

to social chaos since the family, according to the Bible, is the fundamental building block of society.

"This is right" shows that obedience is based on God's command. Obedience to parents is also part of the general revelation of God's will placed within everyone's conscience. Most of the world's cultures place a high priority on children obeying their parents. But for the Christian child, obedience is based on the solid foundation of what Paul has said before: a strong, functioning church and parents committed to Christ and each other.

The Christian child demonstrates reverence to Christ by obeying parents "in the Lord." Within that context, obedience is the way to joy and the avenue of fulfillment. Respect, love, and honor will flow freely, easing families through life's pressure points.

The authority of the wife is also expressly stated here: "Children, obey your parents." In some of the strong patriarchal cultures, a wife had little say in family affairs. But that is not to be the situation in the Christian family.

6:2, 3   Paul quotes the Fifth Commandment, stating that it was the first to give a promise (Deut. 5:16). The child who obeys can expect to have a happy, well-ordered life. The respect that a young child learns to give parents is a first step to learning respect for God, our Heavenly Father. Therefore, respect for one's parents is not just a natural and moral obligation, but a spiritual principle as well.

6:4   William Barclay tells us that a Roman father had absolute power over his own family. He could do as he pleased—make the children work in chains, sell them as slaves, punish them as severely as he chose. He could even inflict the death penalty.

The Christian father, by contrast, should be gentle, meek, self-controlled; a patient educator of his children in the things of God. John Stott assures us that though the word is "fathers," the exhortations are for both parents. Christian parents are to be filled with a knowledge of the Word of God. This is not to be simply an intellectual understanding, but a living faith the children can see daily. Christian parents must understand that their supreme task is rearing their children in the ways of the Lord. In fulfilling this responsibility, parents depend upon the Lord to work in the hearts of their children through them. Thus children are led to a personal relationship with Christ and grow into spiritual maturity.

Work Relationships (6:5-9)

Slavery is a dehumanizing institution, but slaves could sometimes buy their freedom (I Cor. 7:21 and Philem. 16). Though the Stoic philosophers urged masters to show kindness, slavery was inherently against Christian ideals. The seed for the ultimate abolition of slavery is implanted in Paul's commands to Christian slaves and masters, because he treats both as human beings equally answerable to God. The commands Paul gives slaves and masters apply to employer/employee relations in our day.

6:5-8 Slaves (employees) were to obey their earthly masters (employers) in the same way they obeyed Christ. This again goes back to the overarching command in verse 21, "Submit to one another out of reverence for Christ." Paul reminds the Christian slaves repeatedly that Christ is their real master. Therefore, their service should be wholehearted, given with respect and sincerity of heart. Workers should give their all, rather than putting on a false show of enthusiasm when the boss is watching.

Paul encourages these first-century slaves, whose work was often menial, that the Lord rewards people for their proper attitudes and actions. Whether one is slave or free, the Lord sees and compensates the good that person does. The earlier commands against stealing apply here, for employees can easily rob their employers by not working hard or long enough. We would all think twice about stretching our lunch hours if Jesus were our boss. The reality, Paul teaches, is that He is!

6:9 Masters must treat their slaves as Christ has treated them. They are not to be harsh, even though Roman law gave them total control. As fellow members of the Body of Christ with their slaves, they were to respect them as people, not to view them as chattels. Both slave and master report to a higher master in Heaven, the Lord Jesus Christ. He loves them both equally as members of His Body and accords no status differences. All who belong to Christ are heirs of God's promise. The Lord shows no favoritism of rank in His new community: men, women, Jews, Greeks, slaves, masters are all one (see Gal. 3:28, 29).

For Discussion

1. Do you put your marriage partner's concerns first? What steps could you take to improve?

2. How consistent have you been in giving your children spiritual training? What would it take to be more consistent?

3. Do you work as if Christ were your master? How would obedience to this principle change your work habits? Give some examples.

13

Prepared Citizens

Truth to Apply: With the proper Christian armor, I can be victorious in my daily spiritual battles.

Key Verse: Put on the full armor of God so that you can take your stand against the devil's schemes (Eph. 6:11).

Military protective gear has always been crucial to a soldier's well-being. The United States Army spent thousands of dollars to redesign their soldiers' helmet. The new helmet sits lower and covers more of the surface area of the head. Uniforms are often printed with camouflage colors so soldiers can blend into the scenery. Helmets have webbing for inserting brush and leaves. Sturdy, high-lacing boots protect the feet from rough terrain, snakes, and animals.

As a "Christian soldier" do you really believe you have adequate resources to do spiritual battle? What is your past experience in this area?

Background/Overview: *Ephesians 6:10-23*

The final three chapters of Ephesians exhort us to conduct our lives worthy of the calling we have received (Eph. 4:1). Chapters 4 and 5 give many commands relevant to all individual Christians. Chapter 6 gives commands to social units—Christians in a family and Christians at work. Paul ends Ephesians with instructions to all Christians about how to be good soldiers for Christ.

The Christian's battle is not against "flesh and blood" (Eph. 6:12) but against evil spiritual forces. The Bible asserts the reality of spirit beings. They are creatures of God, called "angels." It makes no attempt to prove their existence but assumes it throughout. The historical books often show us angels in action—portraying them as rational, moral, and immortal beings (see Ps. 148:2, 5; Mt. 8:16; Lk. 24:39; Acts 10:22; and Rev. 14:10).

Note that the angelic world consists of both good and evil beings. The evil angels are said to be "fallen" because they have sinned against God (Jude 6; II Pet. 2:4). Some commentators believe Satan, their head, was the highest archangel who led the angelic host in worship of God. But in an attempt to gain this praise for himself, he incited many other angels to follow him in rebellion against God. According to this view, Isaiah 14:12-21 and Ezekiel 28:12-19 have a double reference to an earthly king and to Lucifer (who became Satan).

Light on the Text

The Enemy (6:10-12)

Paul points to the Lord as the source of the strength Christians need to lead a victorious life. Paul's second prayer, in Ephesians 3:14-21, taught that it is through this power at work in us that God does "immeasurably more than all we ask or imagine" (vs. 3:20). Paul often gave the command to be strong. He wrote to the Corinthians, "Be on your guard; stand firm in the faith; be men of courage; be strong" (I Cor. 16:13). He exhorted his beloved Timothy, "You then, my son, be strong in the grace that is in Christ Jesus" (II Tim 2:1).

6:11   The urgency of Paul's appeal should, therefore, be clear. His call to put on God's armor is vital because the believers' enemy (Jn. 10:20) is superior to them. To put on the "full armor," or "panoply" of God, is ultimately to put on the Lord Jesus Himself. Paul told the Roman Christians to "clothe yourselves with the Lord Jesus Christ." (Rom. 13:14). Isaiah 59:17 gives us the imagery of God Himself going forth to battle wearing the breastplate of righteousness and the helmet of salvation.

The Greek word *panoplia,* translated "whole armor," meant the complete outfit soldiers needed for battle. Incomplete armor is little better than no armor. If one part is undefended, that is where defeat will come. The Christian must draw on all the resources available in Christ in order to take a stand against the Devil's schemes. Paul wrote, "We are not unaware of his schemes" (II Cor. 2:11). Only God's provision can enable Christians to frustrate Satan's wicked plans. Jesus provided the model for His followers by quoting Scripture when Satan tried to tempt Him to sin (Mt. 4).

6:12   Here the enemy forces are clearly described. They are not "flesh and blood," but the ruling forces of "this dark world" and the "spiritual forces of evil in the heavenly realms." God has allowed Satan and his evil angels some power over the earth. When Satan showed Jesus the kingdoms of the world, he must have had some substance to his offer. Earlier in this letter, Paul wrote that his readers had followed "the ways of this world and of the ruler of the kingdom of the air" (Eph. 2:2). When a person becomes a Christian, enslavement to Satan is broken, but Satan still desires to make the believer ineffective for God.

John White, in his excellent book *The Fight* (InterVarsity Press), discusses four ways "His Infernal Majesty" attacks Christians: 1) He entices them to sin (Jas. 1:13-15), playing on a Christian's desires. 2) He accuses the Christians (Rev. 12:10), bringing about feelings of guilt for sins Christ has forgiven. 3) He is the deceiver par excellence. 4.) He is also the devourer

(I Pet. 5:8), seeking to ruin those who are trying to live for God, or to silence them by using the fear of death.

The War Uniform (6:13-17)

To withstand the attacks of Satan and his forces, Christians must put on the whole armor of God. The starting point for this picture is probably the Old Testament imagery describing God Himself in martial terms (Isa. 49:16, 17). But Paul would have been well acquainted with the typical military gear of his day. Remember, he was chained to a soldier in Rome while he wrote Ephesians! (For Paul's other uses of the armor imagery, see Romans 13:12; I Thessalonians 5:8.)

The "day of evil" is best understood as the time of temptation, whenever that may come to us, or any felt crisis of the soul's resistance (Eph. 5:16).

Paul pictures a Christian soldier as ready for hand-to-hand combat with the enemy. His armor is complete—sufficient for victory. Each of the six pieces has a distinct purpose. A believer must "put on" each one.

6:14

First, the belt of truth. To the Oriental world, "girding the loins" meant gathering up long, flowing garments by means of a girdle, or belt. This was an absolute necessity for speed and agility. Thus, a soldier had to "tighten his belt" to be prepared for battle. In addition, the belt held the breastplate and sword in place. The belt around the waist signaled that a soldier was on duty. Christians must always be on duty, "making the most of every opportunity, because the days are evil" (Eph. 5:16).

Ephesians 4:14, 15 contrasts the deceitfulness of false doctrine with the truth. Ephesians 4:21 states, "the truth . . . is in Jesus." These verses lead us to believe that the belt of truth means truth personally received. This piece of armor stresses the importance of God's written Word, for it is the source of our truth.

Second, the breastplate of righteousness. This may refer to the holy lives believers are to lead. Without such a life a Christian warrior is defenseless against the accusations of Satan. An unholy life can have no effect on the forces of evil and will influence no one for Christ.

100

6:15 Christian warriors are told to have their feet fitted with "the readiness that comes from the gospel of peace." Both Isaiah 52:7 and Romans 10:15 say the bearers of God's Good News have beautiful feet. Every Christian can be a messenger of God's Gospel, ready to fulfill this responsibility to others. Note that the Gospel is a "gospel of peace": Christ is "our peace," and His death, which broke down the barriers between humanity and God, is described as "making peace" (Eph. 2:14-17). This peace keeps us stable in the midst of conflict.

6:16 The fourth piece of equipment is the shield of faith. A large body shield served as a movable protection against any blows or missiles thrown at a soldier. Faith in God meets Satan's lies with confidence in what God has spoken. Faith believes that God will do what He has said, regardless of adverse circumstances.

In the battles of New Testament times, darts or other missiles were dipped in combustible material, set on fire, and hurled at the enemy. The evil one sends his fiery darts against Christians every day. The shield of faith extinguishes as well as stops them. I John 5:4 promises, "This is the victory that has overcome the world, even our faith."

6:17 An important change in the verb occurs here. Up to this point, Christian warriors must pick up the armor and put it on themselves. The last two pieces they must "take" from God's hands. Just as David rejoiced, "O Sovereign Lord, my strong deliverer, who shields my head in the day of battle" (Ps. 140:7), so Christians rejoice in the assurance of victory over sin through the Cross of Christ. In I Thessalonians 5:8, Paul refers to the helmet as the "hope of salvation." The joy of salvation, freedom from condemnation, and fellowship with God give a Christian warrior the ability to face the enemy.

Finally, Christians are to take the "sword of the Spirit, which is the word of God." Hebrews 4:12 also compares the Word of God to a sharp, deeply penetrating blade. Through the struggle of battle, as a believer looks to God, the Spirit (using and agreeing with the written

Word) may give a customized word to the warrior. When the Word is spoken in faith, the doubts cannot stand.

The Ultimate Weapon (6:18-20)

Paul drops the military comparison to speak directly of a crucial weapon Christians must use in the battle against evil: prayer—unceasing intercession before the Father.

Four "alls" in these verses reveal the comprehensive nature of the Christian soldier's prayer life:

1. "All occasions" tells the when of prayer.
2. "All kinds of prayers and requests" shows the variety of prayer.
3. "Always keep on praying" reveals the manner of prayer.
4. "All the saints" are the objects of prayer.

6:19, 20

Paul specifically asks for prayer for his own boldness in spreading the Gospel. The end of Acts shows that this prayer was answered. Prison didn't stop his proclamation of God's Good News. Rather, Paul truly was "an ambassador in chains" sharing the Gospel with the soldiers who kept watch and with all who visited him while he was under house arrest. The last verse in Acts says, "Boldly and without hindrance he preached the kingdom of God and taught about the Lord Jesus Christ."

Final Greetings (6:21-23)

As was customary, Paul ends his letter with a few personal words. Tychicus, whom he calls a dear brother and faithful servant in the Lord, was no doubt the one who would carry this letter to the Ephesian church. In Acts 20:4, Luke notes that Tychicus was an Asian. Tychicus may have even been from Ephesus since he is listed in that verse along with Trophimus (who, we learn in Acts 21:29, was from Ephesus).

Paul's final words are a blessing that echo the blessings with which he opened his letter: peace, love, and grace.

These words are a synopsis of the great themes of this letter—the peace that Christ's death wrought, the grace God lavishes on us, and the love of Christ that surpasses knowledge.

For Discussion

1. Are you consciously taking up all the armor that God provides, or has apathy or depression sidelined you? How will you begin to appropriate these resources?

2. Is it really possible to have fearlessness in evangelistic encounters? What has been your experience?

3. Do you consistently pray for the concerns of other people beyond your immediate family? How might you become better informed about others' needs?

Leader Helps and Lesson Plan

General Guidelines for Group Study

*Open and close each session with prayer.

*Since the lesson texts are not printed in the book, group members should have their Bibles with them for each study session.

*As the leader, prepare yourself for each session through personal study (during the week) of the Bible text and lesson. On notepaper, jot down any points of interest or concern as you study. Jot down your thoughts about how God is speaking to you through the text, and how He might want to speak to the entire group. Look up cross-reference passages (as they are referred to in the lessons), and try to find answers to questions that come to your mind. Also, recall stories from your own life experience that could be shared with the group to illustrate points in the lesson.

*Try to get participation from everyone. Get to know the more quiet members through informal conversation before and after the sessions. Then, during the study, watch for nonverbal signs (a change in expression or posture) that they would like to respond. Call on them. Say: "What are your thoughts on this, Sue?"

*Don't be afraid of silence. Adults need their own space. Often a long period of silence after a question means the group has been challenged to do some real thinking— hard work that can't be rushed!

*Acknowledge each contribution. No question is a dumb question. Every comment, no matter how "wrong," comes from a worthy person, who needs to be affirmed as valuable to the group. Find ways of tactfully accepting the speaker while guiding the discussion back on track: "Thank you for that comment, John, now what do some of the others think?" or, "I see your point, but are you aware of . . . ?"

When redirecting the discussion, however, be sensitive to the fact that sometimes the topic of the moment *should be* the "sidetrack" because it hits a felt need of the participants.

*Encourage *well-rounded* Christian growth. Christians are called to grow in knowledge of the Word, but they are also challenged to grow in love and wisdom. This means that they must constantly develop in their ability to wisely apply the Bible knowledge to their experience.

Lesson Plan

The following four-step lesson plan can be used effectively for each chapter, varying the different suggested approaches from lesson to lesson.

STEP 1: *Focus on Life Need*

The opening section of each lesson is an anecdote, quote, or other device designed to stimulate sharing on how the topic relates to practical daily living. There are many ways to do this. For example, you might list on the chalkboard the group's answers to: "How have you found this theme relevant to your daily life?" "What are your past successes, or failures, in this area?" "What is your present level of struggle or victory with this?" "Share a story from your own experience relating to this topic."

Sharing questions are designed to be open-ended and allow people to talk about themselves. The questions allow for sharing about past experiences, feelings, hopes and dreams, fears and anxieties, faith, daily life, likes and dislikes, sorrows and joys. Self-disclosure results in group members' coming to know each other at a more intimate level. This kind of personal sharing is necessary to experience deep affirmation and love.

However you do it, the point is to get group members to share *where they are now* in relation to the Biblical topic. As you seek to get the group involved, remember the following characteristics of good sharing questions:[1]

1. Good sharing questions encourage risk without forcing participants to go beyond their willingness to respond.

2. Good sharing questions begin with low risk and build toward higher risk. (It is often good, for instance, to ask a history question to start, then build to present situations in people's lives.)

3. Sharing questions should not require people to confess their sins or to share only negative things about themselves.

4. Questions should be able to be answered by every member of the group.

5. The questions should help the group members to know one another better and learn to love and understand each other more.

6. The questions should allow for enough diversity in response so each member does not wind up saying the same thing.

7. They should ask for sharing of self, not for sharing of opinions.

STEP 2: *Focus on Bible Learning*

Use the "Light on the Text" section for this part of the lesson plan. Again, there are a number of ways to get group members involved, but the emphasis here is more on learning Bible content than on applying it. Below are some suggestions on how to proceed. The methods could be varied from week to week.

*Lecture on important points in the Bible passage (from your personal study notes).

*Assign specific verses in the Bible passage to individuals. Allow five or ten minutes for them to jot down 1) questions, 2) comments, 3) points of concern raised by the text. Then have them share in turn what they have written down.

*Pick important or controversial verses from the passage. In advance, do a personal study to find differences of interpretation among commentators. List and explain these "options" on a blackboard and invite comments concerning the relative merits of each view. Summarize and explain your own view, and challenge other group members to further study.

*Have class members do their own outline of the Bible passage. This is done by giving an original title to each section, chapter, and paragraph, placing each under its appropriate heading according to subject matter. Share the outlines and discuss.

*Make up your own sermons from the Bible passage. Each sermon could include: Title, Theme Sentence, Outline, Illustration, Application, Benediction. Share and discuss.

*View works of art based on the text. Discuss.

*Individually, or as a group, paraphrase the Bible passage in your own words. Share and discuss.

*Have a period of silent meditation upon the Bible passage. Later, share insights.

STEP 3: *Focus on Bible Application*

Most adults prefer group discussion above any other learning method. Use the "For Discussion" section for each lesson to guide a good discussion on the lesson topic and how it relates to felt needs.

Students can benefit from discussion in a number of important ways:[2]

1. Discussion stimulates interest and thinking, and helps students develop the skills of observation, analysis, and hope.

2. Discussion helps students clarify and review what they have learned.

3. Discussion allows students to hear opinions that are more mature and perhaps more Christlike than their own.

4. Discussion stimulates creativity and aids students in applying what they have learned.

5. When students verbalize what they believe and are forced to explain or defend what they say, their convictions are strengthened and their ability to share what they believe with others is increased.

There are many different ways to structure a discussion. All have group interaction as their goal. All provide an opportunity to share in the learning process.

But using different structures can add surprise to a discussion. It can mix people in unique ways. It can allow new people to talk.

Total Class Discussion

In some small classes, all students are able to participate in one effective discussion. This can build a sense of class unity, and it allows everyone to hear the wisdom of peers. But in most groups, total class discussion by itself is unsatisfactory because there is usually time for only a few to contribute.

Buzz Groups

Small groups of three to ten people are assigned any topic for discussion. They quickly select a chairperson and a secretary. The chairperson is responsible for keeping the discussion on track, and the secretary records the group's ideas, reporting the relevant ones to the total class.

Brainstorming

Students, usually in small groups, are presented with a problem and asked to come up with as many different solutions as possible. Participants should withhold judgment until all suggestions (no matter how creative!) have been offered. After a short break, the group should pick the best contribution from those suggested and refine it. Each brainstorming group will present its solution in a total class discussion.

Forum Discussion

Forum discussion is especially valuable when the subject is difficult and the students would not be able to participate in a meaningful discussion without quite a bit of background. People with special training or experience have insights which would not ordinarily be available to the students. Each forum member should prepare a three- to five-minute speech and be given uninterrupted time in which to present it. Then students should be encouraged to interact with the speakers, either directly or through a forum moderator.

Debate

As students prepare before class for their parts in a debate, they should remember that it is the affirmative side's repsonsibility to prove that the resolve is correct. The negative has to prove that it isn't. Of course, the negative may also want to present an alternative proposal.

There are many ways to structure a debate, but the following pattern is quite effective.
1. First affirmative speech
2. First negative speech
3. Second affirmative speech
4. Second negative speech
(brief break while each side plans its rebuttal)
5. First negative rebuttal
6. First affirmative rebuttal
7. Second negative rebuttal
8. Second affirmative rebuttal.

Floating Panel

Sometimes you have a topic to which almost everyone in the room would have something to contribute, for example: marriage, love, work, getting along with people. For a change of pace, have a floating panel: four or five people, whose names are chosen at random, will become "experts" for several minutes. These people sit in chairs in the front of the room while you and other class members ask them questions. The questions should be experience related. When the panel has been in front for several minutes, enough time for each person to make several comments, draw other names and replace the original members.

Interview As Homework

Ask students to interview someone during the week and present what they learned in the form of short reports the following Sunday.

Interview in Class

Occasionally it is profitable to schedule an in-class interview, perhaps with a visiting missionary or with someone who has unique insights to share with the group. One person can take charge of the entire interview, structuring and asking questions. But whenever possible the entire class should take part. Each student should write a question to ask the guest.

In-Group Interview

Divide the class into groups of three, called triads. Supply all groups with the same question or discussion topic. A in the group interviews B while C listens. Then B interviews C while A listens. Finally C interviews A while B listens. Each interview should take from one to three minutes. When the triads return to the class, each person reports on what was heard rather than said.

Following every class period in which you use discussion, ask yourself these questions to help determine the success of your discussion time:

1. In what ways did this discussion contribute to the group's understanding of today's lesson?

2. If each person was not involved, what can I do next week to correct the situation?

3. In what ways did content play a role in the discussion? (I.e., people were not simply sharing off-the-top-of-their-head opinions.)

4. What follow-up, if any, should be made on the discussion? (For example, if participants showed a lack of knowledge, or misunderstanding in some area of Scripture, you may want to cover this subject soon during the class hour. Or, if they discussed decisions they were making or projects they felt the class should be involved in, follow-up outside the class hour may be necessary.)

STEP 4: *Focus on Life Response*

This step tries to incorporate a bridge from the Bible lesson to actual daily living. It should be a *specific* suggestion as to "how we are going to *do* something about this," either individually, or as a group. Though this is a goal to aim for, it is unlikely that everyone will respond to every lesson. But it is good to have a suggested life response ready for that one or two in the group who may have been moved by *this* lesson to respond *this week* in a tangible way.

Sometimes a whole group will be moved by one particular lesson to do a major project in light of their deepened understanding of, and commitment to, God's will. Such a response would be well worth the weeks of study that may have preceded it.

Examples of life response activities:

1. A whole class, after studying Scriptural principles of evangelism, decides to host an outreach Bible study in a new neighborhood.

2. As a result of studying one of Paul's prayers for the Ephesians, a group member volunteers to start and oversee a church prayer chain for responding to those in need.

3. A group member invites others to join her in memorizing the key verse for the week.

4. Two group members, after studying portions of the Sermon on the Mount, write and perform a song about peacemaking.

Obviously, only you and your group can decide how to respond appropriately to the challenge of living for Christ daily. But the possibilities are endless.

[1]From *USING THE BIBLE IN GROUPS*, by Roberta Hestenes. © Roberta Hestenes 1983. Adapted and used by permission of Westminster Press, Philadelphia, PA.

[2]The material on discussion methods is adapted from *Creative Teaching Methods*, by Marlene D. LeFever, available from your local Christian bookstore or from David C. Cook Publishing Co., 850 N. Grove Ave., Elgin, IL 60120. Order number: 25254. $14.95. This book contains step-by-step directions for dozens of methods appropriate for use in adult classes.